Awaken Children

Volume 5

AWAKEN, CHILDREN!

*Dialogues With
Sri Mata Amritanandamayi*

VOLUME 5

Adaptation & Translation

SWAMI AMRITASWARUPANANDA

Mata Amritanandamayi Center, San Ramon
California, United States

AWAKEN, CHILDREN!
Volume 5

Published by:
Mata Amritanandamayi Center
P.O. Box 613
San Ramon, CA 94583
United States

In India:
www.amritapuri.org
inform@amritapuri.org

In Europe:
www.amma-europe.org

In US:
www.amma.org

This Book is Humbly Offered at the
LOTUS FEET OF HER HOLINESS
SRI MATA AMRITANANDAMAYI
The Resplendent Luminary Immanent
In the Hearts of All Beings

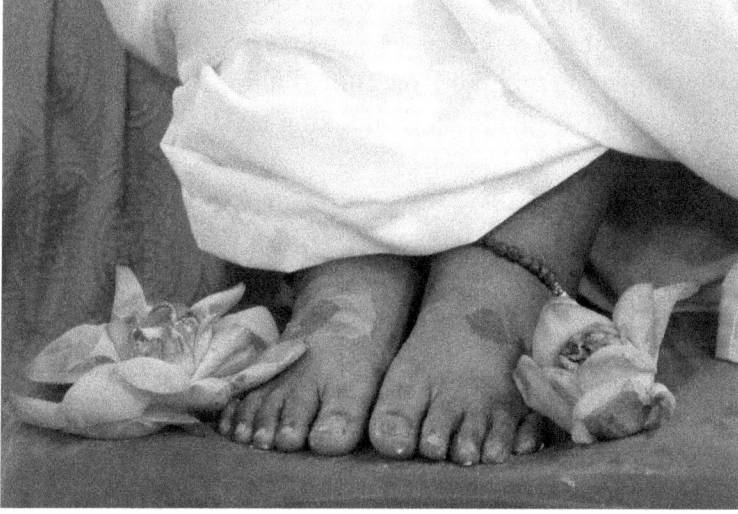

Vandeham saccidānandam bhāvātītam jagatgurum |
Nityam pūrnam nirākāram nirgunam svātmasamsthitam ||
I prostrate to the Universal Teacher, Who is Satchidananda (Pure
Being-Knowledge-Absolute Bliss), Who is beyond all differences,
Who is eternal, all-full, attributeless, formless and ever-centered
in the Self.

Saptasāgaraparyantam tīrthasnānaphalam tu yat |
Gurupādapayōvindōh sahasrāmsena tatphalam ||
Whatever merit is acquired by one, through pilgrimmages and
from bathing in the Sacred Waters extending to the seven seas,
cannot be equal to even one thousandth part of the merit derived
from partaking the water with which the Guru's Feet are washed.

Guru Gita, verses 157, 87

Contents

Introduction   8

Chapter 1   11
   Work with love   13
   Heart and intellect   15
   Stillness of mind   23
   Praying and crying to God as meditation 26
   Spirituality is giving up then taking up 40

Chapter 2   49
   Which is the right attitude?   49
   Forget in order to remember God   65
   Love and reason   68

Chapter 3   77
   Sadhana and destiny   79
   Act with discrimination   88
   Penetrate below the surface   91
   Do not add to your ego   94
   The witness   99

Chapter 4   109
   The beauty of work through love   113

Chapter 5   127
   Discrimination   130
   Compassion makes a mahatma take a body 134

Chapter 6   141
   Be courageous   142
   Response as opposed to reaction   146

Chapter 7   161
   The ability to respond while living in the world 162
   Love and compassion   174

Chapter 8   **189**
   Surrendering   191

Chapter 9   **199**
   Spirituality is real wealth   201

Chapter 10   **205**
   Necessity of the Guru's grace   205
   A Guru's warning   212
   Forget the past   216
   The wonderful healing touch of Amma   225

Glossary   **231**

Index   **236**

Introduction

AUM vāṅg me manasi pratiṣṭhitā
man me vāci pratiṣṭhitam
āvirāvīrma edhi

Om! May my speech be rooted in my mind,
may my mind be rooted in my speech;
Brahman, reveal Thyself to me!

This is how the Upanishadic Rishi prays before he starts speaking about the Supreme Truth. This might be the prayer of all Great Souls. Ever established in that Supreme State of Fullness, they do not want to speak. They know that speaking will distort Truth. Therefore, the Great Ones always prefer to remain in silence.

Yet out of compassion for those who are in search of God and for those who are groping in darkness, the Sage speaks. He knows that he is going to try to do the impossible. Therefore he prays, "O Self-illumined Brahman, I am going to try to put my experience of the Truth into words. It is so full that words cannot express my experience of the Infinite Truth. Still, I am going to try. But when I speak, let me be able to express and convey the Truth, the essential message, through my words. Let me not distort Truth."

Yes... Our Beloved Guru and God, Amma—Mata Amritanandamayi Devi—may also have thought along these lines before speaking. Amma says, "One cannot speak when one is at rest in one's own Self. That is why Lord Dakshinamurti, the first Guru, is always depicted as remaining in silence." But beyond compare is Amma's compassion for Her children. From that State of Perfection from which there is no return, where mind and speech cannot even begin to reach, Amma came down to our level of understanding so that She could share Her experience of the Truth with Her children.

Just like the heavenly Ganges flowing down from the peaks of the Himalayas, bathing and purifying all those who come into Her waters, Amma, with Her arms outstretched, is patiently waiting for Her children to fall into them and to have a glimpse of that Supreme Experience. Once we fall into that warm and heart-soothing embrace, She will slowly help us soar to the unimaginable heights of spiritual bliss.

Sitting on the protective wings of Amma's universal love and compassion, we can listen to Her nectarous, thought-provoking words of wisdom. Each word, each glance and every thought is a profound experience and needs meditation to understand its meaning deep within. If we are able to read this book, every word of it, with that meditativeness, it will always remain as an ever fresh and noble experience in our hearts. Let us try sincerely and see what happens.

In Kerala the monsoon was at its peak. The heavy rains flooded the intricate system of the backwaters, occasionally causing them to overflow. The gigantic waves of the Arabian Sea beat upon the narrow strip of land just off the southwest coast of India. This island was Amma's birthplace, and on the family property Her Ashram was established in 1981, as disciples and devotees found their way to this spiritual haven. To live with a *Mahatma* like Amma is living in consciousness, living in love. Each moment with Her leaves many fragrant memories, creating a chain of unforgettable events and fond remembrances to cradle in the secret, silent chamber of one's heart. No doubt this chain of divine memories will in turn eventually create incessant and unending waves of love, the fuel with which to transcend the downward pull of the world. Just to be with Her is to open the book of divine knowledge and wisdom. This book, however, is not to be read with the mind or the intellect, but read in the silence of one's heart.

Chapter 1

Monday, 2 July, 1984

By eight o'clock in the morning, the night's rain had abated somewhat, but dark clouds still hovered overhead. The Ashram grounds were flooded from the early morning downpour. Except for the thunderous roar from the ocean, the Ashram was quiet and serene.

Because of the rain, the previous night's Devi Bhava had not been as crowded as usual and had ended by one o'clock instead of four or five in the morning. A man who had come to Bhava darshan was sitting on the temple veranda. By his side was a small, old wooden box which looked like a cage. One of the residents approached him and asked if he needed any help. The devotee, a Muslim, replied that he would like to see Amma, even though he had just had Her darshan the night before. As they walked together across the grounds, the man told the resident that he was from Chertalla, a town about 60 kilometers away. He was in the perfume business and earned his living by selling the perfume that he himself made. A week earlier he had come to Karunagappally, a town very near the Ashram, in order to sell his perfumes. There he had heard about Amma, and that very same day he had come to the Ashram for the first time. Since it was a Sunday, he received Amma's darshan during Devi Bhava and returned to Karunagappally, where he spent the night in a mosque. In the middle of the night he had an unusual experience, which he proceeded to tell the resident.

"I was awakened by the sound of somebody opening my perfume box, this box that I have right here by my side. Startled, I jumped and sat up in bed. I was struck with wonder as I beheld Amma looking through my perfume box. She was just as I had seen Her in Devi Bhava. Seeing the startled look on my face, Amma smiled and said to me, 'Son, Amma was searching for pure sandalwood extract. But there is none here.' She then threw me a quick glance and an endearing smile and disappeared. I was left feeling very sad that I could not give Amma what She wanted. So yesterday, I came with the sandalwood extract and sprinkled it over Her during Devi Bhava. Amma seemed very happy and I too felt blissful doing that. She even exclaimed, 'Oh, you brought it.' From that remark it was clear to me that She knew what had happened that night in the mosque. A surge of devotion arose in my heart and my eyes were filled with tears."

The innocent perfume seller had a big smile on his face. He continued, "I feel that my life's goal has been fulfilled. Now before I go, I would like to see Amma once more and bow down at Her Feet. That is why I am still here."

Just at that moment the Holy Mother appeared on the balcony of Her room. The Muslim devotee stood up and bowed down in front of Her with all humility. Mother said to him, "Oh son, are you still here? Have you had something to eat?"

He answered, "I stayed behind to see You once again before continuing on my sales journey. By seeing Amma I have had my food."

Amma laughed and remarked, "Son, you are speaking profound words."

The man answered joyfully, "I am speaking the truth."

There is nothing special about pure sandalwood extract for a Mahatma, who is beyond all desires and who is established in the state of supreme detachment. It is not that the Mahatma wants to have an object like that. He does things like this to create a circumstance so that we will be inspired. Such experiences also instill faith and devotion in our minds. They serve as a ladder for the devotee to ascend slowly toward his goal.

A brahmachari approached to tell Mother that he would not be able to go for the morning meditation because he had some important work to do.

"All right, son," Amma said to him. "Go to the meditation hall and explain to all the others the reason for your absence. Only after doing that can you go and attend to the work. If you are absent without an explanation, others will be tempted to break away from the discipline. Whatever you do, you should try to set an example for others; you should serve as an inspiration to your brothers. Every action of a spiritual seeker should carry a message and a lesson for others. There should be an ideal behind each and every act of a true seeker."

The brahmachari prostrated to Mother and went to the meditation hall. Mother once again expressed Her love and affection to the Muslim devotee and retraced Her steps to Her room.

Work with love

Later in the day at about 2 o'clock, Amma came to know that the cows had not been fed. She felt very sad about the animals being tied to their stalls, and summoned the brahmachari who was in charge of feeding them. As he approached Mother, he hung his head and confessed that he had simply forgotten to feed the cows. With great astonishment Amma exclaimed, "What! You forgot to feed those poor creatures that cannot speak to express their hunger and their thirst? Do you, yourself, ever forget to eat or drink? We humans can ask for food when we are hungry, but they can't, can they? This is a great sin. A spiritual seeker should be able to know the feelings of others—not only the feelings of other people but of all creatures. Don't think that because they are unable to express themselves verbally as humans do, other creatures do not have feelings like humans.

"To be able to put oneself in another's position, to be able to see and to feel as another person does, this is the rare gift of an earnest spiritual seeker. Know that these creatures also have feelings. To provide food and drink for them at the correct time, knowing that they, like us, feel hunger and thirst, is a sadhana. Do not feed the animals mechanically. Don't do it just because it is one of the jobs assigned to you. It must not become mere routine. Try to see that the life that pulsates within you and I is the same life that pulsates within the cows. Try to feel their hunger and thirst, then the work will become a sadhana."

After saying this, Amma Herself took the fodder from a sack in the storeroom and started preparing the food and water for the animals. With great hesitation and fear, the brahmachari approached Mother and requested Her to let him feed the cows. Amma turned to him and said, "Don't say anything now. Mother wants to do this with love. Let these animals feel love in their food."

The brahmachari stood next to Amma apologizing profusely and pleaded with Her to be allowed to feed the cows, but Amma did the work without paying any attention to him. As She fed the cows, Amma caressed and rubbed each animal on the face and forehead with great love and compassion. The animals showed their gratitude by rubbing their heads against Mother's shoulder. There was a smile of contentment on Mother's face. When the cows finished the mixture of water and feed, the Holy Mother walked over to a nearby haystack, and pulling out some hay from the heap, She offered it to the cows. After once more rubbing and caressing the animals, Amma returned to the Ashram. Only after feeding the cows did She eat that day. It was nearly 4:30 p.m. when She had Her lunch.

There is always a special charm and beauty in whatever Amma does because of the tremendous amount of love She pours into every act. We do not know how to love. There is no love in our actions, and therefore, no beauty in what we do. We are always anticipating the fruit of our actions; the result is restlessness and lack of concentration. A one-pointed mind and a selfless attitude are very important in order to imbue one's work with love. If these are absent, love is not possible.

Heart and intellect

At about five o'clock in the afternoon a small crowd of people had gathered on the front veranda of the meditation hall. In the heart of this gathering was Mother, surrounded by the brahmacharis and householder residents of the Ashram, all experiencing the blissful state of singing the Divine Name. Amma sang the lead and the group responded to *Kamesha vamakshi*

> *Salutations to Shakti, the Great Goddess*
> *Who is accessible through devotion;*
> *Salutations to the Seed,*
> *The One Truth,*
> *Infinite and Perfect Awareness.*
>
> *O You, who are the left eye of Shiva*
> *Fulfilling all desires*
> *And shining through all that is animate*
> *and inanimate,*
> *O my Kamala, Ruler of all,*
> *Protect us*

Goddess of the celestials,
Protect them from all sorrows.
O Pure One,
Protect even the Lord of the Ocean of Milk (Vishnu).
The Creator does His work due to Your glance.
Salutations to You who came forth from Brahma,
As Saraswati, the Seed of the entire Universe.

After the song there was a meditative atmosphere for a while. When Mother looked at Her children with an inviting smile, one of the brahmacharis asked, "Amma, this afternoon while you were feeding the cows, I heard you tell the brahmachari not to speak, that you wanted to do the work with love so that the animals could feel it. I didn't understand the real import of what you said, but it sounded to me that there must be some connection between love and speech. Could you please explain?"

Amma replied, "Son, you are not wrong, but the real connection is not between love and speech. The real connection is between love and silence. When there is real love, there is silence. There cannot be any words—there is only stillness. Just like a perfectly calm lake, there cannot be any ripples or waves when real love is experienced. Ripples and waves are a distortion, a distraction, a disturbance in the mental lake. Love ensues from stillness of mind. In that stillness one can experience silence. The talking of the mind stops completely. Real love is felt in that silence. Silence is the only language of pure love.

"Real love exists in the heart. The love that exists in the heart cannot be spoken; it cannot be put into words. The heart is not the place for words. Words are part of the intellect. The intellect can speak, but it is nothing more than a tape recorder; it records and spits out words and words and words—words that don't contain any feelings. The intellect cannot feel compassion; it cannot feel love or kindness. It can only reason. It will even try to reason out love and compassion. Son, where there is too much talking, there is no love. One who really loves is constantly in a meditative mood. Thoughts cease to exist in the presence of such love. The true lover only meditates; he never thinks. All his thoughts are about his beloved, so there are not numerous thought waves in his mind. Only one thought prevails and that singular thought is about his beloved. When there is only one thought, there is no mind. The lover's constant single-minded focus on the beloved touches the innermost recesses of his heart, where words and speech cannot reach. All explanations stop. No more elaboration is possible then. The lover gets drawn into a constant state of meditation. At that point the two become one.

"Meditation prevails in real love. You become silent and remain at rest in your own Real Self. One cannot speak when one is at rest in one's own Self. That is why Lord Dakshinamurti, the first Guru, always remained in silence. It is said that Lord Dakshinamurti taught his disciples through silence. He did not speak, and his disciples did not speak either. But the Lord taught and the disciples understood him.

"But now nobody will understand the silence of a real lover or a meditator. They may consider him strange or call him crazy because the silence of meditation is unknown to them. They are familiar only with words, and the so-called love that they have experienced cannot exist without words. They feel it is impossible to express love without words. However, in that experience of oneness with the beloved, there is no speech. You become silent and still. This state is known as samadhi, a state where you are in constant meditation."

Amma paused for a while and then continued: "There is a story about Lord Shiva and His Holy Consort, Parvati, which will clearly illustrate what is meant by the silence of oneness with the beloved." Thus She proceeded to relate the following story as the devotees listened attentively.

One day Lord Shiva and Parvati were conversing. Shiva, who was always established in the state of samadhi, often wandered about, leaving Parvati alone on Mount Kailash. At a point when Parvati could not bear the pain of separation anymore, She asked Shiva to teach Her how to enter into the state of samadhi so that She could always remain in Oneness with Her Lord. The Lord agreed and instructed His Holy Consort to sit in the lotus posture. He told Her to close Her eyes and meditate, fixing Her gaze within. As Parvati meditated, Shiva asked, "What do you see now?"

"I visualize Your Form in my mental eye," answered Parvati.

Shiva instructed Her further: "Transcend that Form. What do you see now?"

"I behold a brilliant light."

"Now go beyond the light. What next?"

"The sound 'Aum.' That is what I hear now."

"Go beyond the sound. What do you experience now?"

"No answer came to this last question. Her individuality disappeared and dissolved. She became one with Her Lord. In that state there was nobody to speak or listen. She attained the final state of love, the eternal and inseparable union with Her Lord, where the mind with its words and intellectual thinking cannot reach. "

Amma paused at the end of the story. Then She continued, "Whether this story actually happened or not is not important. Try to imbibe the essential message that the story conveys. A person who always thinks intellectually cannot understand the feelings of the heart. He cannot understand the meaning of meditation and love. He knows nothing but talking. What's the use of such an intellect?"

Mother paused and the brahmachari immediately spoke up, "The entire existence of life itself is indebted to the human intellect. What about all the scientific inventions and all the developments of the modern age! They have all been made possible by human intellect. Amma, are you saying that the intellect is useless?"

"Son, try to understand clearly." Mother explained. "Try to be very attentive when you listen to Mother. Remember to use the heart instead of the intellect.

"Children, Mother is not trying to say that the intellect is entirely useless. It is needed; it is absolutely necessary. But it has an appropriate place of its own. Put it where it belongs. Do not use it inappropriately. To place inordinate emphasis on the intellect is dangerous. That will spoil the beauty of life. Too much intellect and not enough heart will cause conflict, disappointment and frustration. There should be a balance between the heart and the intellect. If we penetrate deeply into all aspects of life, we will find that love is hidden behind everything. We will discover that love is the force, the power and inspiration behind every word and every action. This applies to all people, irrespective of race, caste, religion, or profession.

"To an outsider, a scientist making experiments in the laboratory appears to be doing solely intellectual work. Most people will say that his work takes brains, and therefore it is intellectual work and not something that involves the heart. But look carefully into the process. What will be revealed is that there is love in his work, that his heart is engaged in the work. In fact, if you can really see, you will understand that without love one cannot do that kind of work. In reality, the more you observe, the more you will realize that love is the force behind all scientific experimentation and inventions; it is behind all work.

"Love sharpens the intellect. The more love you have, the more sharpness and clarity you will have. You may call it a sharp or subtle intellect, but it is love that is working behind that sharpness or subtlety. It is just a question of realizing this. Some realize it, and some don't."

The brahmachari was listening thoughtfully, but he wanted further clarification: "Amma, I understand, but not completely. Please be kind enough to elaborate a little more."

Amma continued, "Son, no work can be performed without concentration. Whatever the work is, mental or physical, and whether it is easy or difficult, exciting or mundane, concentration is required. Now, what is concentration? Concentration is nothing but stillness of mind. Concentration stops the flow of thoughts. When thoughts stop, the restless mind ceases in its activity and stillness is possible. That stillness of the mind comes only as a result of love. For a scientist it is the love to be inventive and to experiment which helps him dive deeply into his work. He loves to work hard. The common terms used in relation to this are 'interest' or 'sincerity' or 'intense desire.' These terms are synonymous with love. Without love there is no interest, no sincerity or intense desire. Isn't that correct?"

"Amma, in that case, why this differentiation between heart and intellect? They're almost the same thing, aren't they?"

"In the ultimate sense there is no difference at all. But in your present mental state, there is a difference which you yourself impose due to your ignorance. You have not yet reached the Supreme State of Oneness. You are still in the world of duality. You are still in the world of words and phrases—the world of differentiation—hence, this explanation. Once the limitations are surpassed, then there is only love, nothing but Divine Love. In fact, all these explanations and different terms are only to make you understand that experience alone can reveal Truth, and that words and explanations will not do much good.

"When thinking and reasoning predominate in a person, we call him an intellectual. And when there is more love and compassion, we call it heart. Both heart and intellect are needed. In fact, as far as the intellect is concerned, what we really need is not just thinking, but discriminative thinking, a discriminative intellect. We need to be able to think properly and discriminate between good and bad, and we also need a good heart in order to feel and express love. Heart and intellect are necessary for both a sadhak and a person who leads a regular life. Usually, this balance between the heart and the intellect is hard to find.

"Children, love is our real nature. We are of the nature of Divine Love. That love is shining in each and every one of us. As love is our innate nature, there cannot be any manifestation of any kind without this power of love behind it.

"Certainly the scientist who is inventive and who experiments has love in him. But that love is limited to a narrow channel. It is directed only to the scientific field in which he works. It doesn't embrace all creation. He is more or less bound to the laboratory where he sits, or to the scientific equipment which he uses. He does not think of real life. He is more interested in finding out whether there is life on the moon or on Mars. He is more interested in inventing nuclear armaments.

"A scientist may claim that he is trying to find the truth of the empirical world through an analytic approach. He dissects things to analyze how they function. If he is given a kitten, he is more interested in using the animal for research than in loving it as a pet. He will measure its rate of breathing, its pulse and blood pressure. In the name of science and the search for truth, he will dissect the animal and examine its organs. Once the kitten has been cut open, it is dead. Life disappears and any possibility for love is gone. Only if there is life is there love. In his search for the truth of life, the scientist unwittingly destroys life itself. Strange! "Life is love. To see and feel life in everything is love. Life is not on the moon or in the sun. On the contrary, the moon is life, and the sun is life. Life is here. Life is there. Life is everywhere. There is nothing but life. It is the same with love. Wherever there is life, there is love and vice versa. Life and love are not two, they are one. But ignorance about their oneness will prevail until Realization comes. Until Realization comes, the difference between intellect and heart will continue."

There was a deep silence. Everyone's gaze was fixed on Mother's face. She was expounding a profound truth with the greatest simplicity. Everyone sat spellbound until the silence was broken by the flow of Amma's nectarous words as She continued.

"A scientist is more concerned about the outside than the inside. He is more interested in the parts than in the whole. He is so engrossed in the world he perceives, that he is totally unaware of the inner universe. He has many great ideas. He is endowed with a sharp intellect, but his love is limited to the scientific field only. It does not embrace everything. Mother would say that a real scientist should be a real lover—a lover of mankind, a lover of all creation and a lover of life.

"A rishi is a real lover because he has dived into his own Self, the very core of life and love. He experiences life and love every-where—above, below, front, back—in all directions. Even in hell, even in the nether world, he sees nothing but life and love. For him there is nothing but life and love shining forth with splendor and glory from all directions. Therefore, Mother would say that he is a 'real scientist.' He experiments in the inner laboratory of his own being. He never creates division in life. For him life is one whole. He always dwells in that undivided state of love and life.

"The real scientist, the sage, lovingly embraces life and becomes one with it. He never tries to fight with life. While the scientist tries to fight and conquer life, the sage simply surrenders to life and lets it carry him wherever it may."

As She finished the last sentence, Amma entered into a state of samadhi. Her eyes were wide open, but they were still. Her body didn't move at all; it was so motionless that one could not even detect the rise and fall of Her breath. Amma's exalted mood lasted some time. While Amma was absorbed in samadhi, one of the brahmacharis sang a song

Anupama gunanilaye

O Mother, O Goddess,
Abode of unique qualities;
You are the Support of those seeking refuge.
O You who are modest due to Your wisdom,
And gentle, due to love,
Give me a bit of Your compassion.

Even without my saying it,
You know that I don't know enough
To know anything.
Reveal Your Feet and bless me,
for I am falling into the ocean of misery.

Stillness of mind

When She came down to the normal state of consciousness, the same brahmachari asked another question. "Amma, you said that concentration makes the mind still. I have heard that scientific research and experimentation require a tremendous amount of concentration. If so, scientists who spend hours and hours in the laboratory, sometimes even days on end, must experience that stillness of mind. Isn't that true? Is that kind of stillness and the stillness that you are speaking about, one and the same? If not, what is the difference?"

Amma replied, "That is a very intelligent question. Son, though both of them may have a mental stillness, there is vast difference in their experiences. A scientist might experience a certain kind of stillness when he concentrates on a particular experiment or when he is in the process of inventing something. But when he leaves the laboratory, he becomes the same man again. Even though a scientist, he too has vasanas. Controlled by his old habits and vasanas, he will be forced to act according to his mind and desires. He can't remain there in that state of 'no-thought' for long. The scientist can't hold on to the experience of stillness for any great length of time. It simply begins when he enters the laboratory and ends when he comes out. It is true that when a person has one-pointedness, a certain stillness of mind is gained. It can happen even to a layman at certain times. Mother will agree that the concentration is more intense in the case of a scientist than in the case of a layman. The scientist's mind is subtler than that of the layman. The stillness of mind gained by the one-pointedness of the scientist is a special gift, but this kind of stillness does not last long. It comes and goes. It happens when he is in the midst of test tubes and machines, not in his real life. In real life he might be a total failure.

"Children, a rishi's stillness of mind results from the total dropping of the mind. In whatever circumstance he is, the rishi's mind is always still, irrespective of time and place. He goes behind the mind stuff and attains the state of 'no-mind.' The ego dies in him, and thus he is egoless, completely free from the grip of desires. On the other hand, the scientist still carries the burden of ego and still has many desires. Completely emptying the mind, the rishi has fully unburdened the weight of the ego. He is completely free because nothing weighs him down. He is like a mirror, pure and clear as crystal, with no images of its own. If you see any images, they are all reflections, and reflections do not belong to the mirror. The mirror simply reflects. It neither owns nor disowns anything.

"The kind of stillness that you were talking about sometimes happens to a poet when he writes poetry or when he is lost in thought about a theme while looking at nature and weaving his own imaginations. Stillness can come to a farmer as he fantasizes about his crop and the immense harvest that he is going to reap. An ordinary lover who contemplates his beloved can also have the same experience. But these people are all still egocentric. They are still on the mental plane. They are all overburdened. Their heads are full of thoughts, ideas and plans for the future. Once they come out of their so-called stillness, which does not last long, they are once again the same old small ego.

"A scientist keeps adding to his existing ego. He gathers more and more knowledge, more and more information, which only inflates the ego. However, a rishi is completely empty. He becomes like a corpse in a river. He lets the river of life carry him anywhere it likes. The scientist is externally full, full of knowledge about the world. The rishi is internally full—full of the experience of Oneness with the Supreme Absolute. The scientist sees many; the rishi sees One. The scientist is only a part of existence, while the rishi is the whole of existence. While the scientist burdens himself with facts and figures, the rishi becomes empty so that all knowledge can pass through him without affecting his experience of that Oneness. While the scientist limits and narrows his vision, the rishi expands and embraces the entire universe."

Mother stopped talking and asked the brahmacharis to sing

Kodanukoti

O Eternal Truth
For millions and millions of years
Mankind has been searching for You
The ancient sages renounced everything,
Performed endless years of tapas,
To make their Self flow
In meditation
Into Your Divine Stream

Inaccessible to all, Your Infinitesimal Flame
Glowing like the effulgence of the sun
Stands still without even dancing
In the fiercely blowing cyclone.

Flowers, creepers and shrine rooms,
Temples with newly installed sacred pillars,
All are waiting for You
For aeons and aeons,
Yet still You are inaccessibly distant.

Praying and crying to God as meditation

Friday, 6 July, 1984

Amma was giving darshan in the hut. One of the devotees asked, "Amma, I know only a little about spirituality. I have faith in Mother and I want to lead a devoted and dedicated life. Could you please tell me something about becoming more spiritual?"

Mother gave him this answer: "Son, first of all, you should give up the idea of becoming more spiritual. Just try to pray sincerely to God and meditate on Him. Don't think about becoming more spiritual; for that very thought can sometimes be a hindrance.

"Cry and pray to God, and sing His glories. Don't overstrain yourself by trying to sit in lotus posture or holding your breath while meditating on His form. Meditation is remembrance of God, a constant and loving remembrance. Consider Him as your beloved or just consider yourself as His child. Or consider Him as your father or mother. Simply try to think of Him as we think of our father or mother or beloved. How does a lover remember his beloved? Certainly not by sitting in a lotus posture. The remembrance happens spontaneously while he is lying down, walking or sitting on the banks of a river, or it may happen while he is at work. It does not matter where he is or what he is doing. Likewise, remember your beloved deity whenever you can, no matter where you are or what you are doing.

"Contemplate Him as your creator, protector and the final abode to where you will return. Try to feel Him with your heart; try to feel His presence, grace, love and compassion. Open your heart and pray to Him, 'O Lord, my creator, protector, and final resting place, guide me towards Your light and love. Fill my heart with Your presence. I have been told that I am Your child, but I am ignorant of my existence in You. My beloved Lord, I do not know how to worship You, or how to please You, or meditate on Your form. I have not studied the scriptures; I don't know how to glorify You. O Compassionate One, show me the right path, so that I can return to my real home which is nothing but You.'

"Children, pray and shed tears as you think of Him. That is the greatest sadhana. No other sadhana will give you the bliss of divine love as effectively as sincere prayer. You don't have to undergo any academic training to love God. You don't have to be a scholar or a philosopher to worship Him or to call out to Him. Just call out, but let the call come from your heart. Just as a child cries out for food or to be fondled or cuddled by his mother, call out to Him with the same intensity and innocence. Cry and pray to Him. He must reveal Himself. He cannot sit silent and unmoved when somebody calls Him like that.

"Children, innocent prayers, calling out to the Lord, is a powerful way to please the Lord. You don't need to be a scholar to do that. Even for an uneducated layman or an illiterate forest dweller, the Lord's grace can be attained if one is really determined to achieve the goal.

"There is a story which illustrates this point. One of the disciples of the first Sankaracharya was very proud of his devotion to the Lord. His beloved deity was Narasimha, the man-lion, the fourth incarnation of Vishnu. In order to please his beloved deity and to have His vision, the devotee went to the forest to perform intense tapas. For many days he meditated sitting on a rock near the hermitage, and became seriously engaged doing austere sadhana. The sadhak did not notice that one day a forest dweller came to watch him. The forest dweller observed him with great curiosity but couldn't understand why this man was sitting in such an odd position, upright with crossed legs. Since the devotee had his eyes closed, the simple man mistook the meditative posture for sleep. The forest dweller was so curious and eager to speak to the sleeping man, that he came every day and waited for hours, hoping that the devotee would open his eyes.

"At last, a day came when the sadhak emerged from his meditation. The simple forest dweller approached him with great respect and asked, 'Tambra, why do you always sit and sleep? Why don't you lie down?' Seeing the innocence of the forest dweller, the devotee laughed and said, 'Oh, silly man, I am not sleeping. I am meditating on the form of my beloved deity.'

"Of course the forest dweller didn't understand anything. Having lived in the forest all his life, he was uneducated and illiterate. 'Meditating? Beloved deity? What is that?' he exclaimed. The devotee said, 'You do not understand this sort of thing. I am

calling and praying to my Lord.' The forest dweller again won-
dered, 'What! Calling someone without moving from this place?
Why don't you go and look for him?' The devotee did not reply.
He simply smiled and went back into meditation.

"Days passed. The forest dweller's curiosity wouldn't let him
rest. Unable to control his urge to know more about the person
whom the devotee was searching for, he once again approached
the sadhak. With great hope he asked, 'Tambra, who is this
man you are calling? Can I help you find him?' The devotee was
extremely pleased with the man's sincerity. Since he knew that the
forest dweller would not understand anything about meditation
or other techniques of sadhana, the devotee said, 'Look here, the
person I am calling is not a human being but a peculiar kind of
lion, a supremely powerful man-lion.' With this answer the forest
dweller was satisfied.

"The days rolled into months and during this time the two
became close friends. The forest dweller felt sad about his tambra,
who was always sitting in meditation, forgoing food and sleep.
He thought, 'What a disobedient creature this man-lion is! Look
at tambra; he has become so lean and weak for want of food and
sleep. I must do something to help him. That arrogant creature,
who refuses to respond to my tambra's call, must be taught a lesson!' He decided to set out on a journey to look for the man-lion,
but first he wanted to obtain permission from his tambra. The
innocent forest dweller waited for the devotee to open his eyes,
then told him of his intention, asking for permission to go. The
devotee laughed heartily, 'What a crazy, ignorant man! He thinks
the Lord lives somewhere in the forest.' With full conviction that
the forest dweller would meet with failure, but thinking that there
was no sense in trying to make him understand, the devotee gave
his permission. Enjoying the forest dweller's foolishness with great
mirth, the devotee again closed his eyes and went into meditation.

"The forest dweller began his search. He went from cave to cave, from bush to bush, over hills and into valleys. He looked everywhere. Not a single place in the huge dense forest was overlooked in his search for the Tambran's lion. Even after he had searched through all the caves, all the bushes, all the hills and all the valleys, he wouldn't give up. He then began calling out, 'Tambrante simham, va, va.' (My master's Lion, come, come.) He became totally unaware of space and time. Feeling neither hunger nor thirst, he became gaunt like a skeleton. His constant call, 'Tambrante simham, va, va,' echoed everywhere in the forest. It filled the atmosphere, creating a constant and very powerful vibration all around.

"The trees, mountains, valleys, bushes, birds and animals stood still when he called out 'Tambrante simham, va, va.' Even without his knowledge the search had transformed itself into an intense inquiry which slowly had burnt away his primitive nature and along with it all his vasanas. The 'mind stuff' slowly dissolved and all thoughts disappeared; eventually even the verbal calls ceased. He became totally silent. Only the all-consuming fire of love burned within him, and this soared directly up, transcending the celestial abode and finally entering the abode of Lord Vishnu Himself. The flames of this supposedly ignorant forest dweller's meditation were so powerful that Vishnu had to respond. Assuming the form of Narasimha, the man-lion, he appeared before the simple forest dweller.

"The forest dweller pulled out a creeper, tied it around the Lord's neck and led Him back to the tambra who was still sitting on a rock with his eyes closed, trying to see the form of his beloved deity. The forest dweller called out, 'O Tambra, open your eyes. Here is your man-lion. I brought him here for you.' The devotee woke up after repeated calls, and he could not believe his eyes. He rubbed his eyes again and again, looked and looked again. Still he could not believe his eyes. His Lord, the magnificent incarnation of Lord Vishnu, was standing right there before him. With one hand the forest dweller was holding a creeper tied around the Lord's neck, and with the other hand he was feeding Him green grass.

"Seeing how amazed the tambra was, the forest dweller said, 'Tambra, come down. Take your lion. He is all right. He is not dangerous. Come on down.' The devotee scrambled off the rock like an insane man and fell down in front of both the Lord and the forest dweller, crying loudly like a child seeking forgiveness. The forest dweller was puzzled by this. Now the Lord spoke, 'Get up, my dear one. Do not feel disappointed. Remember that dear to Me are those who lovingly remember Me, constantly feeling My presence both within and without. The ego cannot exist where there is real love. Where there is real love, there I can easily enter and dwell.' Having said this, the Lord placed His hand on the forest dweller's head, giving him moksha, final emancipation. The Lord consoled the devotee, saying that he too would reach the ultimate state during this lifetime. The devotee became genuinely humbled.

"The forest dweller had not studied any scriptures, but he had a loving heart. His search was not even for himself but for someone else. This kind of person, endowed with such a loving and compassionate heart, is more dear to the Lord than one who meditates sitting in the lotus posture, proudly contemplating his scriptural knowledge and techniques of meditation and japa.

"Children, taking this story as an inspiration, try to pray until your heart melts and flows out as tears. It is said that the water of the Ganges purifies whoever takes a dip in it. The tears that fill the eyes when one is remembering God have tremendous power to purify one's mind. Such tears are more powerful than meditation. Such tears are verily the Ganges."

Mother always instructs people differently. She sees each being clearly and instructs according to each one's mental caliber and inherited spiritual disposition. Mother advises some to continue on the path that they are following, while She instructs others to do an entirely different form of sadhana. There are cases in which Mother tells a sadhak to continue the same sadhana that he is doing, but with slight changes. Most people who come to see Her are instructed to follow the path of love, devotion, and prayer. Few are those who are told to follow Vedanta, the path of non-duality. According to Mother, most people are not competent enough to perform Vedanta sadhana. Her strong conviction is that Vedanta sadhana will obstruct people's spiritual growth if it is practiced by immature and incompetent people. Mother believes that the number of people who really understand Vedanta and its implications in life is very small.

Amma says, "Vedanta is not something to be talked about. It is a way of life. It is to be lived. Nowadays in the name of Vedanta people get caught up too much in the head, and they destroy all the beauty and charm of spirituality and Divine Love by indulging in egotistic talking and egoistic ways."

The reader may find it strange that Mother should instruct a devotee not to struggle to sit in lotus posture or to hold his breath while meditating. Instead, She will instruct him to cry to the Lord and pray with innocence. Mother says that many people come to Her with the complaint that they have never had a real 'experience', even though they have been performing intense sadhana for several years. Mother believes that this is mainly due to the lack of love and innocence in their sadhana. To really live and to attain real spiritual experience, one must develop the qualities of love and innocence. Amma says that whatever spiritual path one pursues, it should be built on the strong base of *prema* (supreme love) In the case of the devotee who had asked the question, the path of devotion must have been the sadhana which would help him to grow spiritually, since that is what Amma advised him. A real Master knows what is best for his devotees and disciples.

It was nearly six-thirty in the evening. Amma got up and walked toward the temple verandah. It was time to begin the evening bhajan. All the residents and the visiting devotees came and took their seats. Soon the chanting began with the accompaniment of the harmonium and the tabla. Amma sang

Adi Parashakti

O Primal Supreme Power,
Please bless us, rid us of our distress.

O Goddess with eighteen arms,
Whose mount is a lion,
Your eyes are worshipped even by lotus petals,
O You who have a gentle smile.

You have a radiant face
And possess all seven virtues in equal measure.
Your anger is like that of a mad elephant;
You are worshipped by the gods like Ajan.

O Goddess of the Universe,
Dance forever in my heart,
Consider kindly this supplicant,
Granting me all boons.

The blissful moments of singing along with Amma and of experiencing a taste of supreme love and devotion lasted until eight-fifteen. After the arati Amma was found lying in the sand not far from the temple. A few brahmacharis and Gayatri were with Her. Since the sand was wet, somebody brought a mat for Amma to lie on. Gayatri pleaded with Her to lie on the mat, but

Amma did not move. It seemed She was enjoying the wet sand. She started rolling on the ground. Taking this as an opportunity, Gayatri spread the mat on one side hoping that Amma would roll onto it as She was turning back and forth; but Gayatri was disappointed because Amma stopped rolling, and lay still in one spot . Pointing Her right index finger skywards, Amma uttered a number of peculiar sounds, which sounded as if they might be a strange and unknown language. Her extended finger remained in the same position for some time while She lay motionless with Her eyes closed. Several minutes passed before she returned to Her normal mood.

One of the brahmacharis who was present during the afternoon conversation asked, "Amma, this afternoon you instructed a young man just to pray and cry for God. If you want to know God, it that enough?"

"Yes," Mother said, "if it is done with all one's heart. Son, don't think that spiritual practice only entails sitting in lotus posture and meditating or repeating a mantra. Of course, those are also ways and techniques to remember God and to know the Self. They certainly will help to train and tame the naturally restless body and mind. But it is wrong to think that those practices are the only way.

"Take, for example, the gopis of Vrindavan and Mirabai. What was their sadhana? How did they become Krishnamayis (full of Krishna)? Was it through long hours of sitting in a lotus posture doing rigorous meditation? No. But of course they did meditate. They did constant and intense meditation, but not sitting with crossed legs. Devotees like the gopis and Mirabai constantly remembered the glories of the Lord, cherishing His divine form within themselves, irrespective of time or place. They just cried and cried until their tears washed away their entire mind-stuff, until all their thoughts were gone.

"Children, when we cry we can forget everything effortlessly. Crying helps us to stop brooding on the past and dreaming about the future. It helps us to be in the present—with the Lord and His divine leela. Suppose someone very dear to us dies—say our mother or father, wife or husband, or a son or daughter. We will lament, thinking of him or her, won't we? We forget everything else. At that moment nothing else comes to our minds except the sweet memories of the departed one. We will have no other interest than thinking about and contemplating that person. Our minds become fully focused on that person.

Children, crying has the power to make the mind completely one-pointed. Why do we meditate? To get concentration. So, the best way to get concentration is by crying to the Lord. That is a very powerful way of remembering God, and that in fact is meditation. That is what great devotees like the gopis and Mirabai did. See how selflessly Mirabai prayed, 'O Mira's Giridhari, it does not matter if You don't love me. But, O Lord, please do not take away my right to love You.' They prayed and cried until their whole being was transformed into a state of constant prayer. They kept on worshipping the Lord until they were totally consumed by the flames of Divine Love. They themselves became the offering.

"Once you become the offering, once your whole being is in a state of constant prayer, then what is left is not you but Him. What is left is Love. Prayer can perform this miracle. Crying can accomplish this feat. What is the purpose of meditation? It is to become love. It is to attain Oneness. Thus there is no better meditation technique than praying and crying to the Lord.

"Supplicate Him. Pour out your heart to Him. Prayer is nothing but emptying the mind, ridding oneself of the vasanas. Prayer is nothing but accepting His supremacy and remembering your own nothingness. 'I am nothing. I am nobody. You are everything.' Prayer teaches us humility. You are seeking His refuge, His love,

His grace, compassion and help, in order to reach Him. You are calling out, trying to reach out. Prayer is surrendering the ego. From deep within you are trying to reach out. You are trying to become expansive. You tell the Lord, 'O Lord, I have no power. I thought I had, but now I understand that I am helpless. I am in the dark. I cannot see. I am nothing. Guide me, lead me, help me. It was my ego that made me think I was something great. Now I realize that I am helpless. Without Your grace I cannot be anything.' What is this? This is exposing yourself as a totally helpless creature without Him and His Grace. This is humbling yourself. This is the genuine way to exhaust the vasanas. There should be the awareness of helplessness; one should feel one's helplessness. Helplessness will make one humble. Humility in turn will help one get God's grace as well as human love."

Amma was still lying in the sand. She stopped for a while. Nobody spoke for some time. Mother asked for something to drink, but when Gayatri brought it, She didn't drink. Incomprehensible are Her ways. After a long pause, one of the brahmacharis said, "Amma, how does the prayer of a mere believer differ from that of a true devotee?"

Amma answered. "Mere believers, as distinguished from a true devotee, usually pray too. They may use the same terms, and they may engage in the same manner of supplication. In fact the words they use can be identical. But they are just uttering words, meaningless words. They do not truly pray from the heart; they babble. Out of fear or in order to fulfill their desires, they say something, which according to them is prayer. But in reality they are suggesting to God, and even instructing Him, that these are the things they want and those are the things they don't want. They say, 'Give me what I desire and what I like. Do not give those things that I dislike.' How can this be prayer? This is just trying to establish supremacy over God. This is questioning God's omniscient nature. The so-called believer is saying indirectly that he knows better than God what is best for him and what is not. Can we call this prayer? No, we cannot. It is just an exposition of his ego. He still has his own likes and dislikes. His goal is to fulfill his desires. Desire is the central point around which his prayers revolve.

"A true devotee, however, offers himself to the Lord when he prays. Prayer is an offering, an offering of one's own life. Real prayer is real surrender. In real prayer there is nothing to ask, nothing to demand, no suggestions. A true devotee realizes that his Lord is both within and without, that He is all-knowing and all-powerful—omnipresent, omniscient and omnipotent. Understanding this, the devotee simply tries to express his total helplessness to the Lord and accepts Him as the sole protector and guide. In such sincere and open-hearted prayer, the devotee confesses the uselessness and the burden of his ego. Why should one keep a useless thing? Therefore, he prays to the Lord to remove and destroy it. This kind of prayer is real meditation, and it will definitely take one to the goal. In real prayer the devotee has no likes or dislikes. He wants to give up his ego. He tries to see everything as a manifestation of the Lord. He has no other desires to fulfill except to merge in eternal union with his Lord."

Another question was brought up: "Can a person be benefited by someone else's prayer?"

Mother replied, "Yes, that can happen. The concentration, devotion, and pure resolve of the person who prays can affect another person and his desire can be fulfilled. That kind of prayer will work for the fulfillment of a desire, to save someone from danger or to cure a disease.

"But if the goal is to realize the Supreme Being, you should become completely egoless. That requires self-effort. The sadhak himself must pray sincerely for the removal of his negative tendencies. He should work hard. This prayer is not to achieve anything or to fulfill any desire. It is to go beyond all achievements; it is to transcend all desires. It is an intense longing of the sadhak to return to his real, original abode. He feels and becomes aware of the burden of his own ego, and this feeling creates a strong urge to unburden its heaviness. It is this urge which expresses itself as prayer.

"Removal of the ego cannot be attained through the prayers of another limited soul. It takes self-effort and the guidance of a Perfect Master. Working on the ego, or emptying the mind, becomes easier in the presence of a Divine Master. Although Mother has said that somebody else's prayers cannot help remove another person's ego, a Satguru's mere thought, look, or touch can bring about a tremendous transformation in the disciple. If He so wishes, a Satguru can even bestow Self-Realization on His disciple or devotee. He can do anything He likes. His will is one with God's will.

"If you pray for the fulfillment of petty desires, you are stuck to your mind and all its attachments and aversions. Not only that, you are adding more to the existing vasanas. New desires, new worlds, are created. Along with that, you lengthen the chain of your anger, lust, greed, jealousy, delusion, and all other negative traits. Each desire brings with it those negative emotions. Unfulfilled desires result in anger. In contrast to that, when one prays for purification for the purpose of creating *Atma bodha* (awareness of the Self), the vasanas are destroyed. Such prayers will completely change your outlook toward life. The old person dies and a new one is born. However, praying for the fulfillment of petty desires does not involve any change in one's personality. The person who prays in this way remains the same; his attitude remains unchanged.

"This is not to say that you should not be concerned about those who are ill, or those who are less fortunate than you. Pray for them, that the Lord may help them. This is far superior than praying for little petty desires to satisfy the senses. But remember, if your goal is Self-realization, it is your ego, your vasanas, that have to be removed. This needs self-effort and a Satguru's guidance and grace."

After this discussion on prayer, the melancholy tune of the song, filled the atmosphere

Karunatan katamiri

O Mother, kindly cast a compassionate glance at me
That I may attain peace of mind.
I adore Your Holy Feet in the flower of my mind.

Day and night, waves of sorrow
Rise in my mind, overwhelming it.
You are the Ruler of the Earth,
Destroyer of sorrow and Giver of good.

Thus, show Your mercy to me.
O Mother, give me a chance
To adore Your Flower-like Feet.
May Your look of compassion fall on me
That I may become filled with Bliss.

Kindly shower the nectarous drops
Of Your Pure Love on my mind,
Which is miserable and helpless,
Thus letting me bathe and swim
In the cool waters of the Ocean of Bliss.

Spirituality is giving up then taking up

Another question was raised: "Amma, what is the best way in which we can explain spirituality, or interpret it is?

Mother answered, "Spirituality is not something to be explained or interpreted. It is an experience. In fact, to really know what spirituality is, all interpretations and explanations should end. One should be very receptive. There should not be any inner talking or any judgment. All interpretations belong to the head. All interpretations are borrowed ideas or ideas woven out of some other ideas. They are all repetitions. Spirituality can be experienced only in stillness and silence. It is the dropping of all information gathered from the outer world.

"Mother has heard a story. There was a Mahatma who never let others know about his greatness. He always carried around a big sack full of toys and toffees. Whenever he saw any children, he gave them toys and sweets. One day, a team of learned scholars stopped him and said, 'O Revered Holy One, we know that you are a great being. We know you are acting. By carrying around toys and toffees you are trying to put a thick curtain between yourself and us. Please do not delude us. Tell us something about spirituality.

"Immediately when he heard this, the Mahatma dropped the sack and walked a few yards. The people asked, 'What is this? We don't understand the meaning.' The Mahatma replied, 'This is spirituality, unburdening the burden of your ego.' The scholars said, 'All right, what next?' Retracing his steps, the Mahatma picked up the sack and put it back on his shoulder. He said to them, 'This is spirituality: to drop or renounce everything. The heavy sack is your ego with all its negative tendencies, like anger, greed, jealousy, and selfishness. It is a burden. This is the weight that keeps you down. Unburden the weight of your ego. And then, after dropping it completely, you come back and carry it again. But now it is weightless. In other words, don't carry it again until you feel that it is no longer a burden. The ego is then no longer an ego then, but an apparent ego. It is interesting to watch how the apparent ego works. It is just a play. This Self-made ego is here to amuse this one and also those who approach it. This Self-made ego now contains toys and sweets to amuse children.'

"Children, spirituality is nothing but giving up and then taking back. Spirituality is to unburden everything and then take the burden back. But this time the burden is no more a burden. To put it in another way: don't take up the burden until you feel that it is weightless. Yes, when you have completely emptied yourself of the inner burden, you take it back—you carry the burden of the world. But now you won't feel any heaviness. On the contrary, you will feel a tremendous amount of joy springing forth from deep within, even while carrying the burden of the world. Previously, it was real suffering, but now there is no suffering at all, because your mind is fully at rest, and therefore, you do not feel it to be a burden anymore. Even though you still perform actions, you are involved and at the same time not involved. You start seeing things from an entirely different angle. You play a role, but you never identify with it. You remain outside. No matter what you are doing, you always feel blissful."

A comment was made, which revealed some confusion: "To drop the ego and then take it back, and yet remain egoless without feeling the burden of it. How difficult to understand!"

Mother continued: "Amma has said that it is an experience, that it can neither be grasped nor can it be explained or interpreted by the intellect. The intellect has an explanation for every single thing. People are not ready to accept anything without an explanation. They think that there must be a logical explanation for everything. Poor things! They think they can explain the nature of this universe with all its mysteries. Modern scientific thinking is responsible for imparting this kind of attitude to human minds. The modern scientific approach deals only with phenomena and objects that can be perceived. It deals only with the empirical world that can be measured with external instruments, and the conclusions drawn have to be intellectually understandable.

"This concept of modern science has damaged people's faith. Love cannot be perceived, neither can faith. They are not tangible. These qualities cannot be put into words; yet they are the very foundation of life. Without them, life is not life but death. The beauty and splendor of life depend entirely on love and faith. They cannot be explained except in real life. It is our experience that without love and faith, life becomes like a machine or like a corpse. Just as a corpse decomposes, life also starts decomposing in the absence of love and faith. This is our daily experience. Every moment is an experience of this great truth. It is amazing that people still ask for proof and explanations of this. It is a pity that they have such doubts about the truth."

In a split second, Mother once again soared to the heights of spiritual bliss. She was now in a strange mood. She took a handful of wet sand in Her right hand, made it into a ball and placed it on Her forehead. After this, She became very still. Mother closed Her eyes and for some time remained in Her own world, a world totally incomprehensible to the human mind.

Suddenly Mother began singing

Nilameghangale

O dark-colored clouds
How did you get your bluish hue
The same dark complexion
As Vrindavan's Son of Nanda, Sri Krishna?

Did you go and meet Baby Krishna?
Did He smile at you and talk to you?
Did He cast a glance at you
with His blue lotus-like eyes,
Sweet as honey?

The deep silence of the night and the profound elevating feeling created by the song made the minds of everyone glide into a tranquil state. It is indeed wonderful to listen to Mother's nectarous words and ecstatic singing; for She fills both heart and soul with love and contentment. But these intervals of deep silence, when She radiates the bliss of Her own inner silence, are of a beauty beyond words. During these meditative moments, those in Her presence can dive deep, with no effort at all, into the innermost recesses of their own hearts, where they experience silence and peace.

Coming down from Her exalted mood, Mother turned to the side, and the ball of sand fell from Her forehead. One of the brahmacharis carefully picked it up and held it in his hands.

Once again the person who had asked the question about explaining spirituality pursued the same line of thought: "Amma, you did not explain why the saint doesn't feel the burden, even though he is carrying it."

Mother smiled mischievously. She might have been thinking how silly they were to continue to ask the same question even after being told repeatedly that spiritual experiences are indescribable and cannot be explained. However, the Most Compassionate One again blessed Her children by giving a few more hints: "Son, before answering your question, let Mother tell how the intellect keeps on raising objections and doubts. It never lets us believe; it never lets us have undivided faith. Look at you now. Even after you have been told that spirituality is cannot be explained, your intellect doesn't allow you to accept it. It won't allow you to believe. It keeps demanding proof in the form of more and more explanations. This will never stop unless you become aware of how meaningless this repeated questioning is. The more proof and explanations you are given, the more the intellect demands. This is because proof and explanations are food for the intellect. Without doubts, words, and explanations, the mind and intellect cannot survive. They cannot exist. The mind's very source of existence is knowledge from the outside world; therefore it is constantly after facts and figures. Knowing this, try not to feed the mind.

"The saint stops feeding the mind with knowledge of the world. Once food for the ego is stopped, the mind stops its habitual and mechanical functioning. The saint becomes the sole controller. The saint lives in the heart. While the head is the seat of the ego, the heart is the egoless abode. The saint stops living in the head; he leaves the ego and moves to the heart. He does not doubt. He does not divide, but is undivided. He is the universe.

"Once the ego is removed, you are no longer a person. You are consciousness. You are formless. The ego is the material that gives name and form. Once the ego is destroyed, name and form disappear. You may give the saint a name, and you may perceive him as a form, but he is neither. He is like the wind. He is empty space. Everything passes through him. The entire universe—all the suns, moons and stars, the mountains, valleys, and forests, the oceans and rivers, the people and all living creatures—pass right through him; and he simply remains untouched, unmoved, and unperturbed. He lives silently, peacefully, and blissfully. Because he is egoless, he is 'no-mind.'

"Here is another way of looking at it. While remaining under water, we do not feel the weight of the things we carry, no matter how large the quantity may be. But come out of the water and try to carry the same things. You may not be able to move them an inch. Likewise, the Mahatma dives deep into the whole of existence. He becomes existence itself; and buoyant in the space of existence, the 'burden' he carries is weightless. Thus, it is not really a burden that he carries. He feels no burden—for, since he is egoless, he is unburdened.

"A saint lives in love. He lives in compassion. A saint is the embodiment of love and compassion. In pure love there are no burdens. Nothing can be a burden to pure, desireless love. Real love can carry the entire universe without feeling any weight. Compassion can shoulder the suffering of the entire world without feeling the slightest pain. What we call the heavy burden of the entire world is weightless to a Mahatma. He carries this 'burden' out of sheer joy and bliss; but in fact, he does not carry it at all. He cannot carry anything, because he is not a person or a form. He is space itself. He can contain anything. Everything exist within space, and still there is plenty of space left in space. Space is limitless and inexhaustible.

"There is no division in that state; one becomes totally undivided. There is only space. Division is created by us. As a result of our karma, the ego creates division. It is like a house divided by walls into many rooms. Before the house was constructed, there was only space. After the walls were put up, the space was divided into separate rooms. But in reality, even when the house is built and division is created by the walls, there is still only space. The house exists in space. If you demolish the walls, the house disappears, and again you have only space. Likewise, the ego can be compared to the walls that delineate all divisions. Remove the ego and you will again become space.

"But son, what good does it do you, if you simply hear all these words and ideas? You should try to attain that state of being unburdened. Only that is worthwhile."

Another brahmachari felt moved to speak, "It is beautiful when you speak about such things, Amma. Though we are at the lowest ebb of life, we feel so inspired when you speak. Sometimes there is a tide of inner urgency; we feel strongly motivated to know and experience that supreme state. But this feeling does not last long; it soon dies away."

Taking up this point, Mother elaborated, "The tide comes and goes. The tide comes in when you are in situations similar to this, inspired by satsang. The sum total of such inspiring circumstances will culminate in an urgency that will be felt constantly. That will be the take-off point. At that point you will have no choice but to take the final leap, the final soaring upwards. A real Master will take you to that point by creating intense and inspiring situations. As you become more and more receptive, the intensity of the circumstances will increase. That is how a true Guru takes even the most unworthy student slowly and gradually to the goal."

The brahmacharis rejoiced to hear this statement. One of them, considering himself an unworthy disciple, said, "I am happy now, thinking that I too have hope. I am waiting for the day to come when my mind will be filled with the intense desire to merge with Mother."

Mother retorted, "Don't simply wait without doing anything. Do not waste your time just waiting. Utilize the time to prepare the mind, by creating more and more of a gap within so that the Guru can enter. He is always ready to step in, but at least a small crack must be there. Once the Guru has entered, then everything is all right; he will do the rest. He will see to it that you are eaten up. But at present, there is not even a small crack. Try to create an opening, or at least a crack, and allow the Guru to occupy a small space within you. In due course, he will see that the ego is pushed out, so that your entire heart is occupied by him alone."

After these statements, Amma began to sing

Agamanta porule

O Essence of the Agamas, who fills the universe,
Does anyone know You
Who are full of wisdom?
O Blissful Self,
Eternal Being, devoid of sorrow,
O Supreme Primal Power, protect me.

You dwell in all hearts, knowing everyone,
Eager to offer the bliss of Liberation,
Unseen by the wicked,
Yet always shining
In the meditation of the virtuous.

O You, who shines forth
As Eternal Truth,
O Devi, Eternal One,
Illumine the Path of Salvation,
And shine in me, a fool among mankind.

Clearly I tell You, O Mother
Deign to enter and shine in my heart.
Choose me to praise Your story
And liberate me from this maya.

At ten-thirty in the evening it started to rain. It seemed that Mother wished to be in the rain, for She did not get up. As if in tune with Her, everyone remained seated, except Gayatri, who was concerned about Mother's health and physical needs. Gayatri got up, for she could see that the drizzle would soon turn into heavy rain. But Mother did not move. Gayatri pleaded with Mother to get up and move to the temple verandah, or go to Her room. Suddenly the drizzle became a downpour, and everybody got drenched. The moment the drizzle had begun, Gayatri had unfolded the umbrella which she had carried with her, and she tried to hold it over Amma. But Amma was enjoying the rain, and only with much reluctance did She give in to Gayatri's continuous pleading. Finally Amma got up and went along with her to Her room. The brahmacharis stood there a few more moments, as if lost to this world. It took a few minutes for them to realize that Mother was gone. Then suddenly, they all jumped up and rushed to the temple verandah.

One of the brahmacharis, who was shivering, commented, "It seemed to me that Amma wanted to see whether we'd get up and run away when the rain came. Perhaps it was a test. But then again, maybe not. Mother has Her own reasons. Perhaps She simply preferred to stay in the rain."

Another brahmachari said, "I don't know how to act on such occasions. For example, Gayatri insisted that Mother should go to Her room, whereas none of us uttered a single word. We just sat there and kept quiet. Of course we remained in the rain, too. But my question is, which is the right attitude, Gayatri's or ours?"

Sharing these feelings of uneasiness, another brahmachari commented, "Now that you have raised this question, I also have a guilty conscience about it. I think we should have asked Amma to go to Her room before it rained so heavily."

A discussion followed and the brahmacharis concluded that they should ask Mother about it when they had the chance. They then went to their rooms. The only sounds were those of the wind blowing, the rain falling and the ocean waves roaring.

Chapter 2

Which is the right attitude?

Saturday, 7 July, 1984

In the course of the morning the brahmacharis had the opportunity to ask Amma the question that was bothering them the day before. One of them asked, "Amma, yesterday while you were in the rain and it started to pour, Gayatri pleaded that you go to your room, whereas we did not say anything. We just kept quiet. Now, Amma, kindly tell us if it was wrong of us to be silent."

Laughing loudly, Amma replied, "No, no, children! Don't worry, your attitude wasn't wrong. Both Gayatri's attitude and your attitude were correct.

"Gayatri's sadhana is to take care of Amma's physical needs. She is very conscientious about that. The lover, in the beginning stages of love, is always very attached to, and concerned about, his or her beloved's physical body. This attachment, or strong bond, continues until the final state when the lover becomes totally one with the beloved. The attitude of 'I and You' continues to exist in the lover until the final merging takes place. Gayatri is always concerned about Amma's body; Amma's physical needs are what she thinks and dreams about ceaselessly. Her concern for Amma's body arises from her pure love for Amma. That is how it should be—having attachment and deep concern for the Guru's body, even though the Guru is not at all bothered about his own bodily needs. Attachment to the Guru makes one detached from all worldly concerns and worries. It helps the spiritual seeker forget about the world and concentrate on God. The spiritual progress of a disciple or a devotee depends on the intensity of his or her remembrance of his Guru or God, which is also meditation; and this will culminate in total Oneness. Gayatri's thoughts are always focused on Mother and Her needs; there is therefore nothing wrong in Gayatri's attitude. It's fine.

"Children, have you heard the story of Krishna's headache? Lord Krishna one day pretended to have a severe headache. When the sage Narada came into the Lord's private chambers, he saw Krishna rolling on the bed, unable to bear the terrible pain. Expressing great sympathy, Narada inquired if there was anything he could do for the Lord, if there were any remedy to ease his pain. Krishna, as if undergoing severe pain, murmured in a barely audible voice, 'The only medicine is the dust from My devotees' feet. This unbearable pain will disappear only if such dust is applied to My forehead.'

"When he heard this, Narada thought, 'Oh dear! I am the greatest devotee of the Lord; how, then, can I commit the terrible sin of giving the dust from my feet for the Lord to apply on His forehead? That is impossible. I cannot do that.'

"But still he wanted to obtain a cure for the Lord, so he went out and searched for someone who would give the dust from his feet for the Lord to apply to His forehead. First the sage went to Rukmini and Satyabhama, the Holy Consorts of Krishna. They immediately refused, not wanting to commit such a big sin. Next Narada went to see many saints and sages who were renowned for their devotion and tapas, but none of them was ready to commit a great sin like that.

"A disappointed Narada returned to Dwaraka, the abode of Sri Krishna. He told the Lord that those whom he had approached were afraid to incur such a grave sin, and asked where he should go to find the remedy. Seeing Narada's helplessness, the Lord, still feigning severe pain, smilingly replied, 'Go to Vrindavan.'

"So Narada went to Vrindavan, where the gopis were thrilled and excited to see the great devotee of Lord Sri Krishna. They surrounded him, eagerly asking questions about Krishna. After answering their questions, Narada finally told them about the severe headache and its sole remedy, that this was what he had come to ask for. Without a moment's hesitation, and as if they had gone insane, the gopis began filling bags and bags of sand from under their feet.

"Narada was shocked and exclaimed, 'What are you doing? Don't you know that this is the worst sin, to make the Lord wear the dust from your feet? Are you crazy!'

"The gopis in their intense love for the Lord cried out, "Then let us incur this sin, no matter how severe it may be. We don't care. We don't care about sin or merit. Our beloved Krishna's headache must be cured—that is our only concern. If this dust from under our feet will cure His headache, we don't care what punishment lies in store for us. We will gladly accept it.'

"Narada was amazed at the unconditional love and devotion that the gopis had for Krishna. Returning to Dwaraka with the bags of sand from the gopis' feet, Narada found a healthy and fully healed Sri Krishna sitting with a welcoming smile lighting His divine countenance. Narada now realized that the whole headache event was a divine drama played by Sri Krishna to humble him. He was certainly humbled as the Lord said to him, 'My dear Narada, while you and all the others were worried about incurring sin, the gopis were only concerned about Me. They were not at all bothered about what great sin they would incur; in fact, they were willing to accept whatever consequences might befall them for the so-called sinful act of giving the dust of their feet to the Lord. They thought only about Me—that Krishna should be well, and that His pain should end. This was their sole concern. Their bhakti is beyond compare.'

"Children, this attitude of the devotee caring for the Lord's physical well-being is very good. For him, the Lord is both his beloved and his all-in-all; so it is perfectly in keeping with his love and devotion for the devotee to care about the Lord's bodily comforts, His health and physical needs. The devotee's attachment and constant remembrance (one-pointedness) arises out of this attitude, which is very good."

The brahmachari then asked, "Amma, in the beginning you said that our attitude was not wrong, but your explanation makes it sound as if Gayatri was right and we were wrong."

"No, no. Not so," Amma assured him. "Mother was just about to say that your attitude came from a place of being fully identified with that particular set of circumstances. You were in a state of forgetfulness. You didn't see the rain coming; you had not seen the rain clouds gather. Your mind was so concentrated on watching Amma at that particular moment, that even when it started to rain, you did not notice the rain drops. You were living in the moment with Amma, and nothing else mattered. However, since it is Gayatri's sadhana to take care of Amma's physical needs, she was more concerned about Amma's health. She saw the rain coming and was very worried that Amma would get drenched. So, of course, she wanted Amma to get out of the rain and go inside. Both her attitude and yours are correct.

"If Gayatri's attitude can be compared to that of the gopis, who without the slightest hesitation sent the dust of their feet to cure Krishna's headache, your attitude in that moment can be compared to that of the gopi who burned her fingers when she saw Krishna.

"Children, do you know that story? There was once a gopi who was told by her mother-in-law to light the lamp in the house, as dusk was falling. So she went to the neighbor's house to get fire. Back in those days there were no electric lights, not even matches. To light a fire you had to strike a flint, or rub two sticks together; and if somebody did that, he would keep the fire going so that others could start their fires from it. It was a common thing to go to a neighbor's house to fetch fire. The gopi took with her a cotton wick soaked in oil, in order to light it from the lamp at the neighbor's. Just as she placed the oil-soaked wick in the fire, she heard someone say, 'Look, there's Krishna at the door!' She immediately turned and saw her Beloved Krishna standing right there. So struck was she by the sight of her Lord that she simply stood there gazing at Him, unaware of the burning wick in her hand. Totally oblivious to the outer circumstances, she did not notice that her fingers were burning. She felt no pain, for she was not at all conscious of her body. Meanwhile, her mother-in-law was waiting for her to bring the fire; when the daughter-in-law failed to return, the mother-in-law decided to search for her. When she arrived at the neighbor's house, she found the gopi standing entranced, gazing at Krishna. So enchanted was she by His presence, she did not even know that her fingers were burning.

"But remember, this is just an example. You and Gayatri still have a long way to go to reach that state of supreme devotion.

"Children, if you consciously act in a selfish way, that is wrong. For example, if out of anger or spite, you deliberately let Amma stay in the rain, that would be a very harmful attitude, which could adversely affect your spiritual progress. Also, had you run out of the rain without caring about Amma, without seeking Her permission to leave, or without being told by Amma to go, that would have been wrong. However, none of you did any of those things, so don't worry.

"Some people have the attitude that Amma is God, that She is beyond everything and that nothing can affect Her. They think of Her as being all-powerful and know that She can even live without food and sleep, because Her energy is inexhaustible. They consider Her to be the Supreme Brahman, the Absolute. This attitude is also correct.

"The difference is that while a devotee sees both the external and the internal aspects of the Lord, people who believe that God is the Absolute Brahman see only the internal. To you and Gayatri, Mother is your beloved Lord and all-powerful God; She is everything to you.

"Children, Mother knows that you and Gayatri are deeply concerned about Mother's physical well-being; but in that particular set of circumstances, you became identified with the moment and you forgot everything. However, Gayatri was more concerned about Mother's physical body, because that is her sadhana. In both cases, this forgetfulness and identification happens only once in a while. It should become constant—and that is the point when you experience a taste of supreme love."

The brahmacharis were very happy to hear that they had not made a mistake in unwittingly allowing Amma to stay in the rain. This explanation relieved them of any feelings of guilt. As instructed by Amma, one of the brahmacharis sang

Mara yadukula hridayeswara

*O most charming One, Lord of the Yadava's hearts
With the complexion of rain clouds,
Bearing the Goddess Lakshmi on His chest,
O Lotus-eyed One, where are Your fingers
That caress soft lullabies?*

O You who lived in Vrindavan as the son of Nanda,
Who danced and played in the hearts
Of Lord Chaitanya and of others,
You are alpha and omega.
To You who are bonded to Your devotees,
We join our palms in adoration.

At about three o'clock in the afternoon Amma was roaming through the coconut grove. This seemed normal enough, yet there was something unusual in Her manner. One could discern that She was reveling in the higher planes, for the residents had seen Her do this before. It was a particular mood of Hers, abiding in the absolute stillness of Her real nature, while She moved about. This continued for some time.

A few minutes later Mother stopped and looked up at a young coconut tree. Up in the tree an owl was being attacked by a flock of crows. The angry crows screeched wildly as they mercilessly pecked at the defenseless owl. It seemed certain that the crows would kill the owl.

Mother picked up a stone and threw it at the crows, but the crows were not bothered and continued their attack. Mother then picked up several stones and shot them rapidly at the crows. This time the crows accepted defeat and flew away, leaving the owl alone. But soon the poor bird fell down from the tree, fluttered weakly on the ground in front of Mother, and then lay still. There were wounds all over its body. Mother sat down and took the bleeding bird in Her hands, caressing it compassionately. With a sad look on Her face, She gently placed the owl on Her lap. "Gayatri," Mother called out, "bring some hot water and towels."

One of the brahmacharis ran to Gayatri and reported the matter to her. A few minutes later, Gayatri came down from Mother's room with hot water and some towels. Seeing Mother's white skirt covered with blood, Gayatri let these words slip out of her mouth: "Oh dear! Amma, Your skirt is covered with blood. The skirt is ruined."

Mother threw a serious look at Gayatri. The love and compassion She had in Her eyes for the owl was not visible in the look She gave Gayatri. It was more like a warning, as if to say, "Wait till I finish tending to this poor and helpless bird." Gayatri guessed the implications of that look and turned pale.

Using the hot water and the towel, Mother washed the blood from the owl's wounds with great love and concern. She did this with great care, each time washing out the blood-stained towel in a different container. The attention Amma paid to a seemingly insignificant owl was such that everyone present felt as if She were nursing Her own child. Mother did not speak a single word as She treated the bird. When all the blood was removed and the wounds were clean, Mother patted the owl's body dry, using a fresh towel. Then Amma asked Nealu to get some turmeric powder. Nealu quickly returned with turmeric from the kitchen. It was the ready-made type of packaged turmeric powder which had been purchased from the market. But that was not what Mother had in mind: "That's no good," She said. "Get a dried turmeric root, grind it and bring it here."

In a few minutes the freshly-ground turmeric powder was ready, and Mother, with Her own hands, applied the powder on the bird's wounds—under the wings, on the head, around the eyes, and on the neck. She searched carefully to find each wound in order to apply the turmeric powder. As She was doing this, the owl sat silently on Mother's lap without fluttering or moving at all. The owl seemed to be in bliss rather than pain, and it even looked as if it had recovered. Having carefully put the turmeric powder on all its wounds, Amma closed Her eyes and sat in a meditative mood for a few moments, keeping the bird on Her lap. Opening Her eyes, Amma once again rubbed the bird's back.

Then She handed the bird over to Balu and instructed him to take care of it until nightfall. Without moving from where She sat, Amma washed Her hands and remained sitting where She was.

Gayatri reminded Mother of Her blood-stained skirt: "Amma, don't you want to change your skirt?"

As if waiting to hear these words, Amma retorted, "No, Mother does not want to change. She wants to keep the blood on Her clothes. It reminds Amma of the helpless creature and of the pain it underwent. It symbolizes the pain and agony of the entire creation. It makes Her remember the helplessness of those who are in sorrow and are suffering. Thus Mother can remember the need to feel compassion and to express it to all creatures, no matter how insignificant or useless they appear to be. It is very painful for Mother to see how self-centered Her children are. Instead of feeling compassion towards this helpless bird, Gayatri is more concerned about Amma's clothes. It is painful to think that as spiritual seekers, Amma's children do not feel the pain of other beings."

Gayatri hung her head and sat very still. A heavy silence filled the atmosphere and everyone began to feel something of Mother's concern for the entire creation. It was awesome. Tears streamed down Mother's face, but no one knew why. Who can comprehend the meaning of the tears of one so compassionate?

Whenever Mother's mood changes, there is a change in the atmosphere around Her. Her mood is inevitably reflected in the people near Her.

Amma began talking again: "The thought that Her children are not able to feel compassion, that they cannot imagine themselves in someone else's place, is extremely painful to Mother.

"Without love and compassion the world cannot exist. The whole of existence is indebted to the Mahatmas for the love and compassion they have showered on all creation. This creation and all the creatures in it are an expression of compassion. Those who have attained the state of Self-realization do not want to come down. They go beyond. They exist in the beyond. They *are* the beyond.

"That which is beyond is the state of stillness, the state of Oneness. In that state, there is no motion and there is are no thoughts, because there is no mind. For love and compassion to be felt, a mind or a thought is needed, a sankalpa (resolve) is required. So, from the state of 'no-mind,' the state of absolute stillness, a mahatma steps down—perhaps not one, but many steps down—because of his concern for those who are helpless and are groping in the dark. The mahatmas have never wanted to come down. Why should they, when they are one with eternity? Why should they bother about others? Why should consciousness be concerned with the created world? The fact is there are no concerns in that state of Oneness. There are no feelings in that state. There is neither compassion nor lack of compassion. So a mind is created for the purpose of feeling love and compassion, and to be concerned about suffering humanity. By Self-will the Mahatma creates a body through which love and compassion can be expressed. Once compassion arises within, the Mahatma descends to the human plane of consciousness. Why does he do this? What for? Have you ever thought about it? He does it only to create the spirit of love and compassion within you."

Mother stopped for awhile. One of the brahmacharis asked Her, "Amma, it sounds as if you too did not want to come down, as if you would have preferred to remain in that state of Oneness. Then how does this coming down happen? How does that compassion arise?"

Amma, the compassionate one, spoke, "Mother has heard a story about Buddha, about what happened when he became enlightened. Listen carefully.

"Through years of tapas, Buddha became enlightened. When he attained enlightenment, Buddha remained silent for many days. He did not want to speak. He just wanted to lose himself in that oneness with the Supreme Consciousness. So he kept silent. Now, the celestial beings became very distressed. They grew anxious, wondering whether Buddha would ever speak at all. They knew that his enlightenment was a very rare gift; and thus they wanted him to speak so that the entire world and all its creatures could benefit from what he had attained. If he did not speak, it would be a tremendous loss to the world.

"So the gods came down from heaven and appeared before Buddha. Bowing down before the Great Soul, they repeatedly prayed that he would speak. They said, 'Holy One, please speak! Your experience is unique and incomparable; therefore, be compassionate. There are many people who are immersed in pain and sorrow. One single word from you will give them hope. Your mere presence will give them peace and tranquillity. There are also seekers of the Truth who need your help. Guide them to the state of Self-Realization. A word, a glance, a touch from you will be a showering of ambrosia upon them. O Great One, please speak!'

"At first, Buddha, the Enlightened One, paid no heed to their prayers. Then after their continued insistence, he tried to explain to them that nothing he could say would fully express his experience of the Truth. The gods continued to plead with him, 'Think of ailing humanity. Have compassion for those who are in sorrow and despair, longing for someone to give them solace and peace of mind. Think of those seekers of the Truth who are badly in need of someone to guide them to the goal. They need guidance. If nobody helps them, they may look back and think, "I have been waiting for so long to reach the state of Perfection. What if it does not exist? Perhaps there is no such thing as Self-Realization. Why, then, should I waste my time any longer?" And in that state of frustration and disappointment, they might even fall back into the world of plurality. Holy One, think of such people. Take pity on them. Be compassionate towards them and speak. A look, a word or a touch from a holy person like you, is sufficient for them to attain the goal. That attainment of a single soul is enough for the rest of the world to be benefited.'

"Gradually Buddha's heart filled with compassion. And so, after having experienced the highest Truth, after having been filled within and without, and having attained Oneness with the Supreme Being, he came down.

"The prayers and supplications of the gods in this story represent the inner call and longing of sincere sadhaks and people who believe in the existence of a Supreme Power, who are badly in need of God's grace and guidance. There are always such people who yearn intensely for a tangible experience of God. They see the destructive powers trying to overwhelm the higher values of life, and feel the inner urgency for a positive spiritual change. Their intense call and prayers will create waves of compassion in the mind of a great soul. That call compels him to descend."

A brahmachari said, "Amma, I am feeling confused about what you said. Sometimes you say that once Realization is attained one becomes filled with love and compassion, that there is nothing but love in such a person. But I have also heard you say that in that state of Oneness there is neither love nor lack of love, neither compassion nor any lack of compassion. This sounds contradictory. Amma, please make this clear."

"Children," Amma said, "Most of those who attain Realization merge with eternity; very few of them come down. For, who would like to come down after having entered the Ocean of Bliss? In order to come down from that ultimate state, that state from which there is no return, it is necessary to have something to hold on to—a determined thought, a sankalpa. Only a few who can make that resolve to descend will come down. That sankalpa, or mental resolve, is love and compassion, and selfless service to suffering humanity. However, if you do not want to listen and respond to the call of those sincere seekers and the cry of those who are suffering in the world, and if you want to remain in that impersonal state and do not want to be compassionate, it is perfectly all right; you can remain there.

"When you come down, a veil which can be pulled away at any time is put up by Self-will, so that you can function smoothly and uninterruptedly in this world. Consciously, you do not pay any attention to the other side of the curtain. Yet, on and off, you do go over to the other side. But you manage to come back. The very thought or a reminder of the other side can simply lift you there.

"Once you come down, you play your role well. You live and work hard for the uplifting of all humanity. You will have problems, obstacles and difficult situations. You will also have to face abuses, scandals and calumny. But you do not care because although externally you look like everybody else, internally you are different—totally different. Inside, you are one with the Supreme Truth; therefore, you are untouched, unaffected. Having become one with the very source of energy itself, you work tirelessly. Healing and soothing the deep wounds of those who come to you, you give peace and happiness to everyone. Your way of living life—your renunciation, love, compassion, and selflessness—gives inspiration to others to want to experience what you experience.

"If they do not want to be concerned about the world at all, those compassionate and loving ones who come down can also remain in that non-dual state and merge in Supreme Consciousness. In that state there is neither love nor lack of love, neither compassion nor lack of compassion.

"In order to be loving and compassionate, to perform selfless service, and to inspire others to experience those divine qualities, one must have a body. Once a body is acquired, it has to take its natural course. The Mahatma's body is different from an ordinary person's. If he so wills, he can keep the body for as long as he wishes, without being afflicted by disease and suffering. But he consciously makes the body undergo all the experiences that an ordinary human being undergoes. Therein lies his greatness.

"Didn't Krishna get hurt during the Mahabharata battle? Didn't He fight eighteen times with Jarasandha, the cruel and powerful king? Finally, He diplomatically left the battle field. Krishna could have killed Jarasandha if He wanted to, but He didn't. He made Bhima, the second Pandava brother, kill him.

"Remember, it was an arrow shot by an ordinary hunter which put an end to Krishna's life in this world. Jesus was executed on the cross. Both of them could have prevented the events which put an end to their bodies; but they let everything happen in its natural course. They let life carry them. They chose to be as they were and let the events occur. They were willing to surrender. However, this does not mean that the natural course is inevitable or unavoidable for them, as it is for ordinary humans. No, that is not so. If they had wished, they could have averted all bitter experiences. Being all-powerful, they could have effortlessly destroyed those who opposed them. But they wanted to set an example. They wanted to show the world that it is possible to live with the highest values of life, even while undergoing all the problems that ordinary humans have. Yet bear in mind that if a situation arises where it is necessary for them to break a law of nature, they can easily do so. Remember how Sri Rama was about to dry up the entire ocean,[1] and how Sri Krishna lifted up the mountain Govardhana with His little finger."[2]

Amma paused and asked Br. Rao to sing a song,

Muka ganam pativarum

Oh unhappy bees, songs without words,
Won't you come to the Abode of the Divine Mother?

The Divine Mother has come to the world.
No more do we have to wander
On the dusty roads of this earth
The Goddess has come,
With the flowers of spring,
The days that are gone, are gone forever
Now let us go to the Divine Abode.

Let us fill our hearts with new words of wisdom,
filled with the Bliss of the Self,
Let us proclaim that the complex of body and mind
can never be "That."

---

[1] When Sri Rama, an incarnation of Lord Vishnu, reached the ocean and wanted to cross over to Landka to rescue his divine consort, Sita, he prayed to the ocean god to give him passage. Met with indifference, he finally threatened the god who then appeared and gave him passage, and requested that he build a bridge across the water.

[2] In order to humble the proud king of the gods, Indra, Sri Krishna ordered that the annual worship of Indra by the cowherds be offered instead to the mountain, Govardhana. Enraged by this, Indra created torrents of rain to destroy the villagers and their cows. To protect them, Lord Krishna lifted up the mountain and held it aloft on His little finger for seven days and seven nights, during which everyone stayed protected underneath. This is how he got the name, "Govardhana Giridhari," which means, "He who held the hill, Govardhana, aloft.

After the song, Amma continued: "Children, you may attain the highest Truth, but still you may lack compassion. Without feeling love or any concern for suffering human beings, you may remain in the state of Oneness. You will be like a lotus flower blooming on some hidden peak in the Himalayas. Or you will be like a lake full of pure crystal clear water hidden in a deep, inaccessible forest. Or you will be like a fruit tree, full of ripe fruit, in the middle of a dense forest. Nobody can enjoy the beauty and fragrance of that lotus flower; no bee will gather its pollen to make honey. Nobody will come to bathe in that remote lake or drink from it. Nobody can enjoy the sweet and delicious fruit from the inaccessible tree. And yet, your existence is full, clear and pure; for you have reached the goal.

"On the other hand, the compassionate ones, those whose hearts are filled with love and concern, are like a river flowing down from the highest mountain. They are like the Ganges. Having ascended to the highest peak of bliss, they flow down from the heights, out of their compassion, to let others drink from their waters, and bathe and swim in them. They are like a fruit tree growing by the side of the road, offering its fruit to everyone. Tired travelers can enjoy the fruit; they can quench their thirst and appease their hunger. They are like a beautiful lotus blossoming in a temple pond. People can gather around to enjoy its beauty and delight in its fragrance, and doing so, they feel contented. Like bees coming to collect pollen for honey, people will gather around the compassionate ones, waiting for pearls of wisdom to fall from their lips. They themselves become an offering to the people. Such souls have wholly surrendered themselves to all of existence, yet out of compassion, they offer themselves back to the world. Still they remain in silence."

Amma's explanation was so penetrating and revealing that everyone sat absorbed in Her words. Who else could expound so clearly and convincingly about such truths that are "subtler than the subtlest?" Only one who, by Her mere will, can move effortlessly between these two planes of awareness.

One brahmachari spoke up: "Amma, you were talking about your own experience. You were telling us that you came down and assumed this human form just because of your love and compassion for us who are groping in darkness. Amma, how can we repay you for all the trouble that you undergo for us? Amma, how are we to develop this love and compassion? Oh, Amma... Amma... Amma..." The brahmachari started to sob.

Like a mother deeply concerned about her son, Amma consoled him. He slowly stopped crying as She wiped away his tears with Her own hands. It was a truly touching display of Mother's love and compassion for Her children.

Forget in order to remember God

Another brahmachari had a question: "Amma, I have heard you say several times that one should 'forget in order to remember God.' What does that mean?"

Amma explained this seeming paradox: "Children, forgetting is necessary, not only for remembering God. To do any work with concentration, one must forget everything else. While you are studying your lessons, if you start thinking about playing football or about scenes from a movie you have seen, you will not be able to learn. You may read mechanically, but since your mind is elsewhere, the lessons will not enter into your head.

"A scientist forgets all about the outside world when he sits in the laboratory doing research. Several other things may be happening in the same laboratory, but the scientist does not see or hear anything as he attends to his own particular work. He may be looking through a microscope to investigate the cells of the human body, but he will not even be aware of the microscope. He sees nothing but the minute cells that he is studying.

"Thus, in everyday life this kind of forgetting and remembering happens all the time. Each moment something is forgotten and something else is remembered. The family is forgotten and the office is remembered; the wife is forgotten, the children are remembered; the children disappear and the wife appears. This happens constantly, from moment to moment, but we are not aware of it. It is clear that in day-to-day life forgetfulness is required in order to remember something; and the same applies to remembering God. In order to remember God, the world should be forgotten, because, when we see the world, God is forgotten—unless we have the power to see the world as God.

"Constant remembrance of God means a constant forgetting of the world and its objects. A single-pointed remembering increases the gap between two thoughts. We daydream a lot, thinking and brooding about different things, people, places, and so forth. The world exists in us as thoughts and ideas. The world is thought. The biggest impediment to remembering God is thought—our constant thinking and daydreaming, our habit of always trying to figure things out. Our thoughts are always irregular; one thought leads to another. Now we think about our son who lives abroad; we dream about going there and living with him for the rest of our life. Then we dream about that country and the great pleasure and fun we are going to have there. The next moment our thoughts turn to the zoo we visited the other day and the chimpanzees that we saw in one of the cages; the way they jumped from one side to the other; how funny it was when they ate the peanuts we offered, and how they scratched. A moment later we recall our wedding day. This is how most people think. They live in their thoughts.

"If you look carefully, if you can see with a subtle eye, you will see that there is a gap between thoughts. This gap is thin—thinner than a hair's breadth—but it is there. If you can keep the thoughts from flowing uncontrollably, as they do now, this gap will increase. But this is possible only in a mind which is concentrated on a single thought. It must dwell, not on many thoughts, but on just one thought, and that thought is what we call the remembrance of God. That thought can have the name Rama, Krishna, Christ, or Buddha—whatever you call your beloved deity. Through this kind of remembrance, daydreams are forgotten. All other thoughts are dropped, and in due course this remembrance becomes constant. Through constant remembrance of God, one forgets about the world and what is happening. All thoughts are replaced by a single thought: the thought of God. You may call Him Rama, Krishna, Buddha, or Christ. No matter what name you give Him, this one-pointed thinking results in the constant remembrance of God."

The brahmachari was doubtful: "What does one gain from this? What is the benefit of this forgetting and remembering?"

Amma answered, "Suppose you build a beautiful house. It has been your lifelong dream to own such a house. You were always thinking about this dream-home, often forgetting everything else. What do you gain when you finally complete the construction of the house and move into it? You feel happy and content, don't you? Similarly, when you constantly remember God, forgetting all about the world, you will attain peace and perfect contentment. The contentment you experience when you move into your house will die soon, because it will be replaced by another desire, whereas the peace and contentment that you attain through constant remembrance of God, forgetting everything else, will give you eternal peace and happiness.

"What is it that man craves? What is it that is most absent in this world? The answer is peace, isn't it? There is no peace anywhere, neither within nor without. To live life fully, one needs peace and love. Peace is not something that is gained when all desires are fulfilled or when all problems are settled. As long as the mind is there, desires will come up and problems will exist. Peace is something that arises when all the thoughts settle and you transcend the mind. Peace comes when remembrance of God and forgetting the world are experienced simultaneously.

"A person who has inner peace is relaxed. His life is balanced. He is never overexcited or anxious, and he never grieves about his past. He confronts the situations in life calmly and intelligently, because he has great clarity of vision. His mind and vision are not clouded by unnecessary thoughts. Remember, he will have the same problems in life as other people; but a man who knows that inner peace will confront things differently. His attitude will be different. There will be a special charm and beauty in all that he does. He remains unperturbed in all circumstance that arise in life, no matter what they are.

"Children, learn to remember that you are the Self. You are God's own. Try to forget that you are the body, that you are away from God, or that there is nobody to look after you."

Love and reason

When Amma stopped talking, Br. Pai spontaneously sang a song. Everybody, including Amma, joyfully joined him. They sang

Hariyute kalil

*Without falling at the Feet of God (Hari),
None can extinguish
The fire of sorrow, of transmigration.*

Without bowing forever to the Guru
None will gain the bliss of Liberation.

None can reach the Lord
Without getting absorbed in chanting His Name.
Without merging in the sweetness of devotion,
None can attain the state of Liberation.

He who does not meditate, do japa
Or other practices will not partake
Of the nectar of Bliss.
Without righteousness and compassion
Dharma cannot be performed.

Without renouncing all attachments
The fire of transmigration cannot be extinguished.
Unless jealousy within is removed
God will not come to us.

After the song, a brahmachari made the following comment: "To know God or the Self is a question of utter faith, self-surrender and pure love, isn't it? But intellectuals consider these three things irrational and illogical."

Amma had a ready answer, "So-called intellectuals can never enjoy real life. Love is indispensable in real life. Faith requires love, and love needs faith. Self-surrender also requires faith and love. All these qualities are of the heart, and not the intellect.

"Love, surrender, and faith are almost impossible for a rational thinker, for one who is always calculating and analyzing everything. How can such a person love? There is no logic in love. You cannot analyze love. Love is a feeling, a deep feeling. You cannot see love nor can you touch it. But love can be felt, and feelings are in the heart. For love to exist, a heart that can feel and express itself is needed.

"Children, what would happen if a woman fell in love with a rationalist and asked him to marry her? He might say, 'Wait, I have to think about the whole affair. I must analyze the situation and see whether the marriage would be a success or not. I must be rational and figure it out first.' He might even write an essay analyzing the success and failure of love and married life. Most probably the conclusion would be, 'Love is irrational. There is no such thing as love—it is just imagination. Love cannot exist because it cannot be seen, touched, or smelled; it is therefore an illusion. It is impossible.'

"Love just happens. Nobody thinks about how to love, or when and where to love. Nobody is rational about love. Rational thought hinders love. Love is a sudden uprising in the heart. Love is an unavoidable, unobstructable longing for oneness. There is no logic in this. It is beyond logic. So do not try to be rational about love. It is like trying to find a reason to explain why the river flows, or why the breeze is cool and gentle, or why the moon glows and the sky is so expansive, or why the ocean is so vast and deep, and the flower is so fragrant and beautiful. Analyzing kills the beauty and charm of such phenomena. They are to be enjoyed, experienced, and loved. If you rationalize about them, you will miss the beauty and charm and the feelings they evoke. Sit by the seashore. Look at it. Feel its vastness. Feel how the waves swell and subside. Just experience it, and be amazed at creation and at the creator of such magnificence. What good will it do you to rationalize about the ocean?

"Rationalizing destroys beauty. Constant reliance on logic kills poetry, music, painting and singing. It destroys everything that is beautiful in nature. Poetry, music, painting, sculpture, and singing depend on love. The arts are an expression of the artist. It is his heart which is being expressed in his art. The artist pours himself into his art. He dissolves, and only the poetry exists. Only the music exists. Only love exists.

"Faith and self-surrender belong to the same category as love. Love, faith, self-surrender are all connected and interdependent. They are expressions of the heart. Faith is to believe in something that you feel, something which is not visible or tangible, but is an experience. Like love, faith is also an experience. Faith is something deeply personal and subjective. When one has faith, one knows through one's own experience, and nothing needs to be proven. If there is clear-cut, external proof, then it is not faith, but fact. When facts are available, there is no need for faith. For example, the sun, the earth, plants, trees, rivers, and mountains exist. These are facts. No faith is needed to know that they exist. Their existence can be demonstrated. Faith operates where reason fails. Faith and love are beyond reason. The heart feels and experiences faith and love.

"Science has greatly expanded its areas of inquiry, but still there are many things that the human intellect cannot understand; many things cannot be explained by scientific facts. Even though science has attained previously unimagined heights of achievement, the universe remains a mystery. Though it has developed tremendously, science has not yet grasped even an infinitesimal part of what the universe really is. Isn't it true that science has totally failed to make human beings happy and peaceful? Has science with all its great achievements been able to make humanity more humane? All the technological development and scientific advances that we have achieved are the result of our rational thinking; they are products of the intellect. But the predominance of the intellect has destroyed the quality of life; for it has destroyed love, faith, and surrender to a higher goal in life. It has destroyed beauty. It has only helped to inflate the ego, and the vanity of the ego has become a stumbling block for us."

71

Not quite convinced, the same brahmachari commented again: "It sounds as though Amma is against science and intellectual thinking. Shouldn't we also consider the beneficial things that science and intellectual thinking have contributed to the society? "

Mother's answer was benevolent: "Son, Mother is not against science or intellectual thinking. Mother is not saying that science has completely ruined us, nor is She trying to say that intellectual thinking is useless. Science and the intellectual quest have brought about great achievements for the entire human race; there is no doubt about that. But what Amma wants to convey is that we human beings should not give too much importance to science and rational thought to the exclusion of everything else. They have their place. Keep them there, neither in a higher nor a lower place. Remember that life is not a machine. Life is Consciousness itself. Do not make life mechanical. For example, householder shouldn't act like a scientist, a business executive, or an administrator when he is at home. The family is not a machine, and neither are you. Life is not a machine. Love is needed in the home to make it feel alive. Otherwise, home becomes hell.

"If you are a scientist, let your rational side shine forth when you are in the laboratory or among other scientists. That is fine; you can then make use of that aspect of yourself. But when you go home you should be able to drop that role. When you come home you are returning to your real life, and you should be able to shift from your head to your heart. You should have the strength to stop thinking about your science and experiments.

"In the home you are not a scientist or an engineer; there your work is not the most important thing. Your frowns and serious expression have no place at home. How boring and dry life would be if you went directly to your work room without even glancing or smiling at your wife and children when you came home. Think of the pain and stress this would create in your family life—there wouldn't be any smiling faces. The head of a family who always sits with his chin resting in his palm, who is constantly thinking about his work, is not living up to his duties as husband and father. If he does not interact with his wife and children, tension, stress, and strain will be created, and everyone will find home life boring and sad.

"How many family relationships collapse because of lack of love and concern? How many wives come to Amma saying, 'Amma, my husband doesn't even smile at me. He never speaks lovingly to me. He has no concern for me at all. I find it difficult to live with him. What should I do?' Sometimes such women go after other men, or they become addicted to drugs, or they even commit suicide. In some cases, it is the husband who is the victim. There are countless cases where children are neglected and ignored.

"Children, what Mother says is that you can become whatever you want, but your professional life must be separated from life with your family. You can use you intellect and think as much as you like; but at the same time, you should be able to drop the intellect and embrace love and faith whenever you wish. You should be able to change the frown into a beautiful smile at any time.

"Love creates smiling, laughing faces and compassionate hearts, and is expressed in sweet and pleasing words. You can choose both head and heart. There is no problem in this, but there should be a balance, for if you choose logic and rational thinking alone, you are in trouble. Love will not create trouble. Love eliminates all troubles. In love there is no trouble, no fear, no agitation, no tension or anger. But to rely on rational, intellectual thinking solely, you will find yourself burdened with many problems, and you will be in constant trouble. Remember, the choice is yours. Use your discrimination. Remember, Mother isn't dismissing science and logic. Mother is only trying to point out the dangerous tendency of the modern age to give too much importance to reason and logic, at the expense of love and faith, the qualities that unite the human race."

It was nearly five-thirty in the afternoon. Amma got up from the coconut grove and walked toward the southern end of the Ashram, where the backwaters divided the Ashram property from the neighbors' land. These neighbors were devotees of Mother. Two girls, who were older than Amma, were especially devoted to Her. In the years when there was nobody to look after Amma, these two girls helped to take care of Her. They often brought Her to their house, where they bathed Her and gave Her food. Now, as if they had been waiting for Amma, these girls and their whole family came running to the edge of their property. Between Mother and the family lay the backwaters. Amma was so happy and pleased to see them all together. Calling across the backwaters, She inquired about their welfare. The oldest son told Mother that the fishermen in the area had been having a hard time. Because of the heavy rain and high tide, they had been unable to catch any fish for several days. "What a pity! What will happen to them if this continues?" Amma's sadness was evident as She spoke. "It would be sufficient if they had food for at least one day."

The conversation between Amma and the family continued for a while. At its conclusion the family left and Mother walked back through the coconut grove, Her hands held behind Her back. She stopped when She reached the southwestern corner of the Ashram, and stood there gazing at the sea and the waves, and at a long row of fishing boats perched along the shore.

Mother stood there for some time. Perhaps She was thinking about the misfortunes of the fishermen and their families. Upon hearing of their plight, Amma had immediately displayed deep concern. Having been born and raised in this village, She knew what it meant to go for many days without a good catch. It seemed that the ominous sea serpent of starvation and poverty was raising it hood on the seashore.

During the evening bhajan Mother sang,

Ammayalle entammayalle

Are You not my Mother?
Oh, are You not my dear Mother
Who wipes away the tears?
Are You not the Mother of the fourteen worlds,
Creator of the world?

How many days have I been calling You,
O You whose nature is Shakti,
Will You not come?

O You who love to grant all desires,
Are Creation, Preservation and Destruction not in You?

Mother wept as She sang. Were they tears of bliss, or was She crying on behalf of the poor fishermen, praying to the Supreme Self on their behalf?

After the bhajan Amma called Nealu and said, "Son, Mother is sick at heart hearing that the children on the seashore have no food. Mother must do something, otherwise She will not be at peace. Mother will not be able to eat or sleep. Make arrangements to distribute rice and other foodstuffs to them tomorrow."

"As Amma wishes," was Nealu's reply.

The lights in the Ashram were turned off at eleven o'clock, but at twelve the lights in Amma's room were still on. It was raining, but if one listened carefully through the sound of the falling rain, one could hear the melodious sound of the tamboura coming from Amma's room. In harmony with the gentle sound of this string instrument Mother sang

Kalina kananen kannukal

O dark-colored One,
My eyes are burning pitifully
for the sight of Your Feet.
O lotus-eyed One, come running
with the cows and the music of your flute.

Having no butter or milk to offer You,
I offer You a little of my pain.
O Kanna, at Your Feet
I offer the pearl drops of my tears.

For how many days have I been calling You?
Have You not even a bit of compassion?
What great error have I committed?
Are You not the Lover of Your devotees?

Mother might have been praying for the fisherfolk. The dark night wrapped itself around the sounds of the falling rain, around the roar of the ocean waves and Amma's song. The atmosphere of this rainy night was full of pathos. Drawn outside by Mother's song, a few brahmacharis sat in front of their huts listening. Mother's mood seemed to be a reflection of the distress and disappointment of the fishermen. What else could it be? Her mind which is One with the Universe feels and reflects everything that happens around Her.

Chapter 3

Sunday, 8 July, 1984

Everyone was surprised to see the rising sun this morning. After so many days of heavy rain, it was truly a beautiful sight. The sun's rays danced and sparkled on the wet leaves. Birds chirped gleefully, jumping from one branch to another. The day seemed promising, as if things might now take a better turn for the fishermen. Arrangements were made, according to Amma's instructions, to distribute rice and other foodstuffs to the villagers on the seashore.

The ashramites believed that the change of weather came as the result of Mother's sankalpa to improve the lot of the fishermen and their families. When She had first heard about their distress, She seemed deeply affected, and ceased to eat or drink anything. Her songs were like intense prayers of appeal to save the villagers from starvation. Mother Herself had initially made the statement that they should have food for at least one day. As it was, there was no rain on this sunny day, and most surprisingly, the ocean was not rough as it had been on previous days. The fishermen went out to fish in the afternoon and had a very good catch, which saved many families from starving. Thus Amma's statement about their having food for at least one day came true, both through the distribution of food from the Ashram and by their having a good catch.

Darshan began at around eleven o'clock. As Amma came into the hut, a little boy was walking beside Her. It was Shakti Prasad, a child born by Mother's blessing to a childless couple. Holding on to Amma's hand, the boy looked like a little yogi. Around his neck hung a mala of big rudraksha beads, and there were long, broad lines of sacred ash applied across his forehead. The devotees stared at the boy's appearance. Seeing their looks of curiosity, Amma told them, "He insisted on wearing the big mala and the sacred ash." Amma sounded very happy and pleased with this boy who had come to spend a few days with Her.

Mother sat down on the cot, and remained in a meditative mood with Her eyes closed for some time, as the brahmacharis chanted the

Guru Paduka Stotram

Aum
To You, dear Guru, to Your sandals I bow;
O peerless Guru, to Your sandals I bow.
You are our teacher, the Lord of all powers;
To Your sandals, dear Guru, once again I bow.

Endowed with the power of 'aim' and of 'hrim',
Your sandals contain all the glory of 'shrim'.
The deep inner meaning of 'Om' they expound;
To Your sandals, dear Guru, once again do I bow.

Fire-ceremonies, oblations by priests,
All rites of religion are hereby complete:
The knowledge of Brahman Your sandals bestow;
To Your sandals, dear Guru, I most reverently bow.

An eagle to slay all the snakes of desire,
Dispassion and wisdom Your sandals inspire.

Your sandals give knowledge and liberty now;
To Your sandals, dear Guru, once again do I bow.

A trustworthy boat to cross over life's sea;
Your sandals awake true devotion to You.
They serve as a fire to the waters of doubt;
To Your sandals, dear Guru, once again do I bow.

The brahmacharis continued their devotional singing while Mother gave darshan.

Sadhana and destiny

One of the devotees had a bandage on his forehead, and Mother was anxious to know why it was there. With a mischievous smile on his face he replied, "You know why, Amma. Without You I would not have been able to come here today." The devotee then told Amma that he had had a motorbike accident as he was returning home from work. He had been in a hurry to get home to see his son who was bed-ridden with high fever and was vomiting, he ignored the heavy traffic and drove very fast through the rain. As he wove in and out of the traffic, a truck suddenly appeared in his lane and hit him. The impact of the collision was so hard that the bike rebounded off the truck, throwing the devotee onto the road.

"I thought I was going to be crushed to death by the fast moving vehicles," he told Amma. "Gathering all my strength I called out, 'Amma, save me! Protect me!' Suddenly I remembered my son, and again I called, 'Amma, my son!' Closing my eyes tightly, I waited to be crushed to death under the wheels of a heavy truck, but that didn't happen. Instead, I felt someone's hands carrying me. It seemed as if I were floating or flying in the air, and yet I clearly felt I was being cradled in someone's hands. Opening my eyes, I still felt the hands but did not see anyone. Then slowly a face appeared before my eyes. It was You, Amma! It was You..." The man sobbed and covered his face with both hands. Through tears he said, "I would never have seen your compassionate face again. I would never have seen my son again. Had I died in that accident, he would have been heartbroken and would have died too." The devotee cried uncontrollably.

Like a loving Mother consoling her favorite child, Amma rubbed his back, patted him and stroked his forehead, telling him not to worry as nothing bad had happened. When the man finally calmed down, he wanted to complete his story. He said that he had lost consciousness after seeing Amma's smiling face. When he opened his eyes, he had found himself lying in the meadow by the side of the road, surrounded by a crowd of people. He had been surprised to learn that all of that had happened just within seconds.

He further related, "From people's remarks about how miraculously I escaped, I guessed that they must have seen how the accident happened and how mysteriously I had landed in the meadow. They were about to take me to the hospital, when all of a sudden I stood up saying that I was all right. Except for this wound on my forehead and one on my left knee, I was fine. Last night I had a thorough check-up and the doctors said that I was perfectly well. Amma, you have saved my life." As he said these words, the devotee's eyes again filled with tears.

Mother gently inquired, "How is your son? Is he feeling well?"

The man replied, "By your grace, by the time I finally got home yesterday, his fever had gone down and now he feels much better."

Another devotee who had been listening to the story was prompted to ask a question about destiny: "Can his escape from death be considered the fruit of his actions alone? Is it the result of karma? Was he destined to be saved by you, or was he destined to die?

Mother explained, "This accident was destined to happen and he was destined to die. But Mother warned him months ago that something very serious would happen, and that he should pray and meditate as much as he could. He obeyed and followed all of Mother's instructions. His obedience, sincerity, and devotion enabled him to receive God's Grace. It was that Grace that saved him from death. But remember, a serious accident did happen. It was an experience that he had to undergo, but he was saved. This was the result of his own effort. His sincere and dedicated effort made compassion and grace flow, and this saved his life. Children, even destiny can be overcome by sincere and dedicated effort. In such a person's case, God Himself will alter his destiny."

The devotee who had met with the accident continued: "Five months ago when I first came to have Amma's darshan, She told me that I should be very careful, that in a few month's I would have to face something very serious and dangerous. When Amma learned that I owned a motorbike, She again gave me a warning. She specifically told me that I should always drive slowly. Amma even forbade me from traveling long distances on the motorbike."

The man who had asked about destiny brought up another point, "Amma, you said that this devotee followed your instructions perfectly and that is what made grace flow toward him. But in some cases, these kinds of miracles happen even before people meet you. I have heard many tell such stories. They say that Amma helped them or someone in their family, even though they hadn't met you yet. In cases like these, you did not give them instructions, nor did they perform any sadhana. Can you explain this?

Mother answered: "It is true that some people have experiences similar to this, even before meeting Mother. Son, remember that all those who are associated with Amma in this lifetime were also with Her in their previous lives. You can see only this lifetime and therefore you think they did not know Mother before. But they have all been with Amma before. So you cannot say that those experiences happened before they met Mother. No one remembers or knows his connection to Mother in previous lives. There is a predestined time for each one to come to Mother. Some come earlier, others later. But every one of Mother's children has always been with Her. They come to Mother at different times, they may hear about Amma or may happen to see Her photograph; they may have listened to a recording of Amma's bhajans. In some cases people come to Amma after meeting one of Her children; still others realize their relationship to Amma only through direct contact with Her.

"You talk about 'before meeting Amma,' but there is no such thing. All of Amma's children have already met Amma long ago. Even though no one is aware of it, Amma's protection has always been there. Having followed the instructions given to them in a previous life, people experience God's grace. Even if they aren't following the Guru's instructions or doing sadhana in this life, they may still receive God's grace due to the merit they have acquired in a previous life.

"You will not see Amma giving any instructions to those devotees, because they have already been given instructions. You may not see them following any instructions, for they may have already done so in the past. They have accumulated enough merit in a previous life for the Guru's grace to flow toward them in this life. In such cases the devotee must have done whatever he was supposed to do. Now he is ready for the fruit, because the fruition must come. If the Mahatma decides that the fruit of the devotee's action is to be given on a particular occasion in this life, it will happen. The Guru is the one who bestows the fruit of one's actions. He knows when to give it. You see only a very small portion of life. Remember that this life is only an infinitesimal portion of your total life. Don't evaluate things by looking at this small bit. Furthermore, you see the Mahatma's actions only from the outside, so how can you judge? The Mahatma is the only one who knows everything about the past, present, and future; therefore, you can't make any judgments about the Mahatma, or about whether other people deserve the Guru's grace or not. Once the Guru's instructions have been followed, the results must come to fruition, because it is a debt that Amma must pay, so to speak.

"Son, do not try to judge things before penetrating them. You do not know how to penetrate because you have always been on the surface. To penetrate you need a subtle mind, a subtle eye, and a still mind. A vacillating mind cannot penetrate. Only a still mind can do so.

"Son, you should approach all the devotees who come here; go to all the residents of the Ashram, and ask them about their relationship with Amma. Try to find out when they met Mother and how long they have been with Her. Ask them about their feelings. All of them without exception will say, 'I came on such and such a date. I have been here with Mother for the last eight, nine or ten years.' And they will also add, 'Yet I strongly feel that my relationship with Amma has existed for many lives. I felt this the moment I met Her. Amma, too, acted with such familiarity toward me; She seemed to have known me before.'

"You feel the same way too, don't you? Why? Does this feeling of familiarity exist in every relationship? No, it does not. Usually when we meet someone, getting to know him takes time. Usually there is a feeling that the other person is a stranger to you, and that you are a stranger to him. But none of Mother's children have that feeling with Her. None of Mother's children say that Amma is a stranger to them or that Amma acs like a stranger. Why? Because She has been with you always. Amma has never left you.

"All of you have the experience within you of having previously been with Amma. It lies dormant within you. When the right time comes it will manifest.

"Children, bestowing a blessing or showering grace on someone is totally in the control of a Mahatma. He can do it anytime he wants, or He can refrain from doing it if he doesn't want to. Grace is a strange phenomenon. One cannot say when, where, or how grace will come. Human calculations fail when it comes to matters of grace. If he so wishes, in a split second the Guru can bestow the blessing of Self-realization on a stranger who has not performed any sadhana. He can also hold back from giving it to a person who has been doing intense sadhana for a long time. Mother is not saying that a Mahatma will withhold grace from a deserving sadhak. She is simply emphasizing that it is within his power to bestow it or not to bestow grace. A Mahatma can easily bless someone by fulfilling his lifelong desire. We may try to analyze why a person is so blessed since we may not see any merit in him, but such a search to find a reason or cause will remain a total mystery for us mortal human beings who cannot go beyond the intellect. Sometimes there will not be any cause for it. The Guru simply does it. Therefore, in order to attain this grace, cry and pray, hold on to the feet of the Guru, no matter what happens."

The darshan continued as people moved forward to be enveloped by Mother's loving embrace and pour out their hearts to Her. The devotees sang

Samsara dukha samanam

O Mother of the World
Dispeller of the sorrows of transmigration
The shelter of Your Blessed Hand
Is the only refuge for us.

You are the refuge of blind and lost souls
The remembrance of Your Lotus Feet
Protects everyone from danger.

For the deluded ones
Wallowing in the dense darkness,
Meditation on Your name and form
Is the only solution for their wretched state

Cast a glance at my mind
With Your beautiful glowing eyes,
O Mother, Your Grace is the only means
to reach Your Lotus Feet.

When the song ended there was a brief silence. Then Amma continued talking, "A person's destiny can be changed through the power of a Mahatma, through the workings of a saint. Here is a story to illustrate this:

"There once lived an ardent devotee of Lord Vishnu. After several years of marriage, he and his wife were not blessed with any children. This devotee did intense tapas for the sake of having a child. But the couple remained childless. One day the devotee met the sage, Narada, who was passing through his village. When he learnt that the sage was going to Vaikunta to receive Lord Vishnu's darshan, the devotee begged Narada to ask the Lord why he and his wife were not yet blessed with a child. He also wanted to know when he might expect to have such a blessing.

When he reached Vaikunta, Narada faithfully conveyed the devotee's message to the Lord. Lord Vishnu said that the devotee was not destined to have any children in this lifetime. This was such a disappointing answer that Narada did not want to tell the devotee what the Lord had said. He therefore never communicated this unpleasant news to the man.

"Years passed and Narada once again happened to pass through that same village. He paid a visit to the devotee's house and was very surprised to find three children playing in the courtyard. Upon being told that they were the devotee's children, Narada asked the man how it was that these children came to be born to him.

"The devotee related to Narada that not long after the sage had passed through the village the last time, the devotee was fortunate enough to meet a saint and serve him. 'The saint was pleased with my service,' the devotee explained, 'and he told me to ask for a boon. Of course I prayed for a child and the saint said that I would have three children. That is how these children came into my life.'

"Narada went straight to Vaikunta and accused Lord Vishnu of not speaking the truth: 'A few years ago, when I asked for a child on behalf of a certain devotee, You told me that he was not destined to have any children. Yet, now he has three!'

"Before Narada had a chance to mention anything about the saint, Lord Vishnu laughed and said, "That must be the work of a saint, for only saints can change one's destiny.

"Children, a Mahatma can bestow a blessing which even God cannot. God is nameless and formless; He cannot be seen. A Mahatma gives reality to the existence of God. In His presence, people can see and experience God. The Mahatma blesses people with a tangible experience of God. He makes a great sacrifice by leaving the Supreme Abode of Bliss to live in the midst of ordinary people, like one among them, yet remaining in eternal union."

Another question was brought up: "Amma, some people who were nonbelievers before become ardent devotees when they meet You. How does that happen?"

Mother answered, "Children, it is true that they may be nonbelievers for some time. That is their karma. But at some point they will have to come to believe in God. These people—nonbelievers who very suddenly become ardent devotees after meeting Amma—have been atheists only in this lifetime, because of the circumstances and conditions into which they were born. However, deep within they still possess the spiritual *samskara* (qualities) inherited from previous lives, and that will be predominant. Compared to the atheistic qualities they have accumulated during this life or the previous one, the latent spiritual samskara of a devotee is stronger. When their atheistic tendencies are exhausted, the long-standing faith within them will emerge. It is only a question of time. This unmanifested devotion manifests when they meet a Perfect Master, or when they are exposed to a deeply spiritual situation. At this point the weaker tendencies give way to the stronger spiritual ones. These people will still have to do sadhana under the guidance of a Perfect Master in order to eliminate the accumulated tendencies from this life and previous lives. Remember that they will still have vasanas to work on. The only difference is that the spiritual samskara will be a little stronger than the vasanas. This stronger samskara helps them come closer to a Mahatma or God. But a Mahatma, if he wishes, can also create a great transformation in a nonbeliever who doesn't have any spiritual disposition inherited from the previous life. Nothing is impossible for a Mahatma.

Mother asked the brahmacharis to sing. They sang

Kerunnen manasam Amma

O Mother, my mind is crying
O my Mother, have You no ear to hear it?
With an aching heart, I have wandered
All over the land in search of You.
Why this delay to come before me?
O Mother, what shall I do now?

What sin has this helpless weakling committed
For You to show such indifference to me?
O Mother, I shall wash Your Lotus Feet
With my hot tears.

O Mother, I am tired of this unbearable burden,
The fruit of past deeds.
O Mother, delay not to give refuge
To this utterly exhausted humble servant of Yours.

The brahmacharis sang the song with so much intensity and devotion that Amma entered into samadhi. She sat very still; Her eyes were half-closed. Her hands were held in two divine mudras. There was complete silence for a few minutes as the devotees sat gazing at Mother's face with awe and devotion. The silence was broken as the brahmacharis began chanting Hari Om... Hari Om... Everybody responded. The atmosphere was saturated with divine spiritual energy.

Act with discrimination

Monday, 9 July, 1984

This morning Amma was sitting in the dining hall which was located north of the temple. It was breakfast time and She asked Gayatri to pluck a few leaves from a jackfruit tree. It is customary in the villages of Kerala for people to use these leaves, folded in a certain way, to make a spoon for drinking kanji or any other liquid food. Gayatri went out and came back with ten or fifteen leaves. Seeing so many leaves in Gayatri's hands, Amma exclaimed, "Oh, what a great sin you have committed! I asked you to bring only a few leaves, enough for five people. You have unnecessarily destroyed life. That is a sin. You have done something unrighteous.

How could you do this? An action performed without proper discrimination is adharma. What have you learned after being with Mother for so many years? One will commit such a sin only if one does not have any love or compassion. You could not feel life pulsating in those leaves; therefore, you didn't have any compassion towards them. Lack of compassion makes it easy to destroy life. When you have no compassion, you have no concern for others. This indicates that you have no faith either, because compassion is an extension of faith—faith in the existence of all-pervading life. Such lack of faith and shraddha prompts you to act indiscriminately. By picking many more leaves than necessary, you acted without any discrimination."

There was a pause. Amma looked at Gayatri. She wanted to ask Mother something but was afraid to open her mouth. Amma continued, "Gayatri-mol is thinking, 'How can the plucking of a few extra leaves be adharma, if plucking five leaves is not? How come plucking five leaves is not adharma?'"

Gayatri was amazed to hear Amma say this, for that was exactly what she wanted to ask Amma but was afraid to.

Time and time again a Mahatma's omniscience is revealed. Yet, even people who are closely associated with a Mahatma fail to understand him. They may have had a hundred experiences which fully convinced them of the Mahatma's omniscience and all-pervasiveness, but still occasions arise when they are doubtful. Of course, as Mother puts it, "Complete faith is Self-realization." The power of *Mahamaya* (the Great Illusion) is inexplicable. The thick curtain of vasanas makes it difficult for us to dive deep into the consciousness of the Guru or the Mahatma.

Amma answered Gayatri's thought: "Any action performed without discrimination is adharma, an unrighteous act. It is a sin. Whatever is wasted due to our lack of care and attention is a sin. Everything has been created for a purpose. Everything has a use.

Without the interdependence of things the world couldn't exist. Plants and trees cannot exist without the earth. Animals depend on plants and other animals for food. Human beings depend on animals and plants. Thus the existence of the entire world is nothing but a story of inter-dependence.

"Things meant for human sustenance can be used. If you need only two potatoes, for instance, take two, and not three. Suppose two potatoes are sufficient to cook a dish; if you then take three instead of two, you are acting indiscriminately. You are committing an adharmic act.

"Wastefulness is a form of stealing. Since you are not really using the third potato, you are carelessly wasting it. You could give it to someone else, perhaps to a neighbor who does not have enough to eat. Thus by taking that extra potato, you are denying him food. You are stealing his food, and are committing an unrighteous act.

"Plucking a few leaves, enough for five people, would not have been wrong, but you plucked an extra ten. This changed the whole situation. Your action was adharmic: First of all, you unnecessarily destroyed the life of ten leaves. Secondly, you denied them to someone else. These leaves will be wasted due to your acting without thinking."

One of the brahmacharis said, "Amma is expressing exactly the same principle that Krishna did in the Srimad Bhagavad Gita. Sri Krishna called people who hoard things and do not give to the needy 'stenah,' meaning thieves."

Amma continued, "Exactly. What else can such people be? Those who keep more than they need without giving anything to others, who are badly in need, are really thieves. Their hoarding causes people to rob and steal. Amma has heard of a Mahatma who was made the magistrate of a country. The way he handled the first case brought before him was very strange. He ordered both the thief and the person who had been robbed to be put in jail. When he was questioned by the king about this odd punishment, the Mahatma said, 'The rich man hoarded too much wealth. He neither used it properly nor did he distribute it to those who could. There are many people starving and dying for want of food, clothing and shelter. In fact, the rich man should be grateful to the thief that he was not murdered.'

"Then he added, 'I feel a little guilty because I gave the same punishment to both of them. I should have given a harsher punishment to the rich man, because he is the one who caused the thief to steal. Had he distributed his extra wealth to the poor and needy, this would not have happened.' "

When Mother had finished the story, She continued to sit in the dining hall for a few more minutes, engaged in light conversation. Then She went back to Her room.

Penetrate below the surface

At eleven in the morning Amma was giving darshan in the hut.

As She received the devotees, a brahmachari who was sitting next to Mother asked a question: "Amma, I heard you say the other day that we do not know how to penetrate, that we are always on the surface. You also said that in order to penetrate, a subtle mind and a subtle eye are needed. What do you mean by penetrating? Can you explain?"

Amma answered, "It is the nature of the human mind to vacillate. Just like the pendulum of a clock, the mind always moves from one thing to another, from one mood or emotion to another. This movement is constant. The mind is always in a state of flux. At one moment the mind loves; the next moment it hates. Now the mind likes something, the next moment it dislikes something else. The pendulum of the mind sometimes moves to anger, then moves to desire. It cannot stop; it cannot be still. Because of this constant movement, the stable, unmoving underlying ground of existence, the real nature of things, is not seen. The movement of the mind creates incessant waves, and these waves, the ripples of thoughts, cloud everything, so that nothing can be seen clearly. This movement is like a fog clouding our vision. You see something, but not clearly. You cannot see properly because of the cloud of thoughts. Thus your perception is defective. You make statements about what you perceive, not knowing that your vision is clouded; thus, you make faulty judgments and give out wrong information.

"Each thought, each emotional outburst, and each desire is like a pebble thrown into the waters of the mental lake. The incessant thoughts are like the ripples on the surface of a lake. The undulating surface makes it impossible for you to see through the water clearly. What is at the bottom of the lake cannot be seen properly, for it is distorted by the ripples on the surface. You never allow the mind to be still. Either there is a craving to fulfill a desire, or there is anger, jealousy, love, or hatred; and if there is nothing happening in the present, memories of the past will crawl in. The sweet and bitter memories, the joyful moments, the regrets, the desire for revenge—something will arise. Then when the past withdraws, the future comes with beautiful promises and dreams. Thus the mind is fully engaged; it is always occupied and never still.

"Children, you perceive only the waves on the surface; yet because of this movement on the surface, you mistakenly think that the bottom is moving too. But the ground is still. It cannot move. You are superimposing the movement of the surface—the ripples of thoughts and emotions—onto the still bottom, the underlying ground. The movement belongs only to the surface—to the mind. The movement is caused by thought waves. It has nothing to do with the ground. But to see this immovable substratum, the surface should become still and silent. The ripples have to stop; the vacillating pendulum of the mind must be stilled. This quieting of the mind is what is known as penetration.

"Once this stillness is attained, you can see clearly through the surface. You stop seeing distorted forms. You behold the real ground of existence—the Truth. All your doubts end. At this point, you realize that you have been seeing distorted forms, that you have been seeing only shadows and clouds. It is then that you realize your ignorance. Before reaching this state, you may say that you are ignorant; however, you are never really aware of it. To penetrate is to behold the real nature of everything while constantly abiding in your own Self.

"Look at the eyes of real yogis (saints). They have penetrating eyes. They can see right through you. When they look at you, they are not looking at your illusory, distorted form. On the contrary, they are looking at your infinite being; they are looking at the Self. They don't see you, the ego: they see beyond the ego. They don't see the play; they see the immovable stage on which the play is being enacted. This means that they see the play as a play. They don't give it any reality. The play can stop at anytime, but the stage remains. They watch and enjoy the play but never become identified with it."

Darshan was still in progress at twelve forty-five. The brahmacharis were singing the song,

Mannayi marayum

Man dies and disappears as dust
But is born again on this earth and grows up.

If he does good actions, he may attain
To a higher status, and then return to earth again.

In life one must undergo disease and old age
O man, think! Is it worth being born again and again?
What are all these evil tendencies for?

A person may have done many evil deeds,
But if he knows Who is behind this world,
Then all his negativity will be removed
And he will be immersed in the Ocean of Bliss.

Do not add to your ego

After the song, another question was asked: "Amma, you have said that at some point, we will realize that we have been seeing only illusory forms; that we will experience the real nature of things only when we attain the state of stillness. That is when we will realize our ignorance. What do you mean by realizing our ignorance?

Amma said, "Children, at present everyone is in a state of ignorance. Even great scholars admit that they are ignorant. When people pray or when they are in the presence of a Mahatma, they say, 'O Lord, ignorant as I am, please guide me. I do not know anything. Shower your grace upon me.' These are common expressions used by people who say they are ignorant, but how many really know that they are ignorant? How many are aware of their ignorance? People are not aware. Awareness helps eliminate the ego; but because people are not aware of their ignorance, they cannot remove it. Even if they could understand it intellectually, they would still continue to think that they are great; thus, they are not really aware of their ignorance.

"Ignorance is the ignorance of Reality. The concept most people have of ignorance is different. It is a common belief that an ignorant person is one who has not studied, one who is not learned. Scholars would say that an ignorant person is one who has not studied the Vedas or Upanishads and who has no knowledge of modern science. This is what scholars think ignorance is; therefore, they study. They read whatever books they can get. Once they have become learned they want to speak, they want to teach others and give discourses. They want listeners. They long to be told by others that they are great scholars with such deep insight and wisdom. They want to be adored, and they want to become Gurus. All this, of course, adds to their ego. Their ego was small before they learned so many things. They had less of a burden then. To unload that lesser burden would not have been such a big job, but now the load has become very heavy. Hard work is needed to make even a small crack in a big solid ego.

"Still people like this will pray. Such egotistical people pray, not out of humility or love, but out of fear. While they are praying they use flowery language. In their prayers they beautifully present their ignorance to God. They ask for God's grace to remove their ignorance and to kindle the light of knowledge within them. In front of others they make a display of being very humble. Having given a long discourse, this kind of person will repeatedly say how ignorant he is and pretend to be humble when people applaud or praise him. But within he is happy as his ego becomes more and more inflated; he is overflowing with joy because others think he is a great scholar.

"Such people do not realize their ignorance. They may say they are ignorant, but they don't feel it, for they really believe that they are great. They think their knowledge about the scriptures is real knowledge. For them learning is an ornament, something to acquire and wear as a display. As a result, a person who thinks and acts like this gets an inflated ego. His ego gets puffed up, yet he doesn't feel its weight. It is important that one should feel the heaviness of one's ego. The more one feels that the ego is a burden, the more intense will be the longing to unload it and be rid of it.

"However, most people don't feel that their ego is a burden. They believe it is needed. They see the ego as an embellishment to their personality, that it gives them beauty and charm. Remember, a person may say that he is nobody, that he is nothing; but if you touch his ego, if you point a finger at his ego and expose how identified he is with it, he will erupt like a volcano, and the lava of protests will spill out. He reacts out of his total identification with his ego. How can people like this realize the truth about their ignorance? It is very difficult." Then Mother added playfully, "You need a big sledge hammer to break the ego of a person like this."

Everyone burst into laughter, and Amma laughed too. There was a pause, and then She continued: "This is one of the most important things to understand. One must become aware of how egocentric one is. A person should realize that his ego is a burden; he should be aware of his ignorance. He should know that book knowledge is not real knowledge, that such learning only adds to the strength of the ego, unless one is subtle enough to go beyond the words and see the real truth.

"Even ego-centered people pray, using the same or similar words as real devotees. But their prayers don't come from their hearts. They simply utter the words. Externally they look like great devotees, and they may speak beautifully about spirituality, but they have a strong ego, subtle and hard to break. They may pray and sit in a meditative posture, but within their minds are wandering. Such an attitude is the worst kind of ignorance. Yet, a person who is like this does not realize how ignorant he is."

This brings to mind an incident that happened in 1981. One day Amma was sitting at the edge of the backwaters at the southwestern corner of the Ashram. In those days one could look out beyond the backwaters and get a good view of the ocean. There were a few brahmacharis with Mother, and also some devotees from the neighborhood, and Mother's parents. They were discussing practical matters concerning the Ashram, when a middle-aged, distinguished-looking visitor approached them. After greeting Amma and acknowledging the others present, he sat down and began to tell the purpose of his visit.

"I am on a spiritual journey," he said, "call it a pilgrimage, if you will. I have come to the realization that life is not worth living unless one finds the real meaning of life, the real reason why we are here on this earth. The ancient saints and sages of India all say that we are here to gain the ultimate goal of Self-realization. So now, after having lived a life in which I have been blessed with financial success, I have both the time and the means to satisfy my only passion in life, the spiritual quest."

Thus he continued philosophizing. He spoke eloquently. He sounded as if he wanted to let others know how knowledgeable he was. He seemed to be trying to make others believe how sincere he was in his quest for truth. "As far as I am concerned," he said, "the most important sadhana is meditation. Only in meditation can I establish a real relationship with God, for God knows me more than anyone else, more than I even know myself."

The man continued in this vein for a while as his words were met with slight nods of acknowledgment from those who were present, for he appeared to be well-versed and erudite in what he was saying. Amma sat, smiling at him as She listened.

Encouraged by the relaxed atmosphere, he slowly glanced around and said, "I feel quite at home in ashrams. I have visited so many. Ah, there is such a feeling of peace here. May I stay here for a few days to meditate?" With those words he sat in the lotus posture, closed his eyes and began to meditate.

Br. Nealu now resumed speaking to Amma about certain Ashram matters. After the brief discussion was concluded, Amma got up. Everyone prostrated to Her. The man seemed to be in deep meditation. As Amma passed by him, She placed Her palm fully on the top of his head and gave it a good shake, saying, "Are you still bargaining in that teakwood purchase?" Then She walked on. The man was startled. He was obviously shocked. He couldn't meditate anymore. He stood up looking restless and disturbed. As he walked back and forth, he asked one of the brahmacharis several times if he could have a personal audience with Mother. Just before the evening bhajan, Mother granted his request. It was revealed that this man was a timber merchant dealing in teakwood in the northern part of Kerala. For the last two weeks he had been trying to acquire some very high quality teakwood. He had placed his bid but the seller wanted a higher price than the one he had offered. He was honest and told Mother that just when She had placed Her hand on him to shake him, it was exactly as Mother said: in his mind he was actually doing the bargaining with the seller.

This man felt remorseful about his pretense and asked for Mother's forgiveness. "Amma, now I know you are truly a great saint. You knew all along that I was only speaking from my fantasies about being a spiritual seeker. You have humbled me, Amma. I don't want to be pretentious about spirituality anymore. Oh, Amma, please help me be honest to myself. I know you can help me."

Later, when the man left the Ashram, some of the brahmacharis were discussing this incident, mocking his pretension. When this reached Amma's ears, She scolded them with sharply for being so mean: "Don't feel so great about yourselves. At present you're not very different from him. Who can refrain from brooding when there are so many dreams accumulated within?"

Mother darshan continued as the brahmacharis began another chant of the Divine Name

Devi maheswariye

O Divine Mother, Great Goddess
Whose nature is illusion
O Cause and Creator of the Universe,
I bow to You again and again.

O dark-haired Empress of the Universe,
O great Maya of beautiful limbs,
O Supreme Goddess,
You are the Friend of devotees,
Granting them both bondage and liberation.

You are that merciful Goddess
In whom everything has arisen,
By whom everything is led
In whom everything will merge.

As the singing continued, Mother slipped into an inwardly absorbed state sitting on the cot in the darshan hut. What an incomprehensible phenomenon! Just a few minutes earlier She had been speaking great words of wisdom. All of sudden, without notice, She was gone! She was no more in this world. Silence fell on the crowd and a deep feeling of peace permeated the hut. Inspired by Amma's blissful state, the devotees easily slipped into meditation.

The witness

Having soared to the peaks of spiritual awareness, Mother came back down after a few minutes and resumed giving darshan to the assembled devotees. A brahmachari asked a question: "Amma, you just mentioned that the saint, when he looks at us, is looking at the infinite consciousness, not at the external person. But when the saint speaks to us, he sometimes discloses things about our past and future—things that are related to our physical form. Even you do this, Amma. How can the saint speak like this without seeing our external form? "

Mother responded, "Again Amma says that the saint sees only the infinite Self, not the person. Yes, he may speak to you; so what? When he speaks to you, he is only a witness. He speaks only because it will benefit you. You are inspired by his words, and through his words you are given a glimpse of reality. Otherwise he prefers to be silent. He is silence. When a saint speaks, he doesn't really speak; his body speaks and he witnesses it. When the saint sleeps, he does not sleep; he watches the sleep of his body. When he works, he is not working; he merely observes the body working. He is simply a presence, a constant presence, a witness to all that happens to his own body and all around.

"If the saint is sick, he comes out of his body and looks at the great pain that it undergoes. If he is insulted or abused by others, again he comes out of his body and watches; he witnesses the trouble the body is undergoing. Then he can laugh at the insults showered on him. He can laugh at the angry looks and words directed toward him. He is no longer the body; he is Pure Consciousness. How can consciousness get angry? How can consciousness be insulted? It's impossible! The saint is consciousness, thus he is untouched and unaffected by insults or anger.

"When the saint looks at you, he does see your form, your physical appearance; not because your body is in front of him or because his eyes are wide open, but because he wants to see your form. If he does not want to see you, he won't. He is the master of his mind, not a slave to it. We are the ones who are enslaved by the mind.

"If the saint looks at you and sees your form, it is only because he wishes to see your form, but he can also stop seeing you even if you are sitting in front of him and his eyes are wide open. If he discloses your past, present and future, what of it? Why is that so astounding? If he wishes, he can tell you about the past, present, and future of the entire universe, because he is the universe. The universe is within him. The universe is like a bubble within his existence. To look at the universe and to make a few predictions is not difficult for him. He is the ocean of existence, and the universe is like a bubble or a small wave within him. If he tells you something about yourself, he still remains a detached witness to what he is saying. But usually he doesn't bother with disclosures of this sort. He does not engage himself in talk of what happens in the world. He is constantly in meditation.

"Now the word meditation should not be misunderstood. Do not compare your meditation with the saint's. Your meditation is not meditation. Your meditation is constant effort, a struggle to attain the state of meditation. But the saint is always in this state. Whether he walks, sits, sleeps, eats, or talks, he is always in deep meditation. There is no time when he is not meditating, when he is not abiding in his own Self.

"Thus, because the saint abides in his own infinite Self, he sees the infinite Self in all others. It is not a contradiction to say that he sees another person's form, for he does so only if he wishes. He can enter his body and join in the play, and he can withdraw at will. He can let the senses see, speak, eat, run, laugh or sleep, but he can withdraw them anytime he wants. Whatever he does, the Mahatma continues to abide within his own Self, beholding everything as his own Self. Never does he become identified with his body—he simply observes. He is constantly watching. As he watches what takes place around him, he can let his body take part in it and withdraw at will. But even when he is taking part in it, he is not involved at all. However, he knows that the only reality is the infinite Self. "

Mother stopped for a while, and the devotees sat in silence, taking in what She had just said. The silence was broken by a devotee, an elderly man, who said: "Amma's words remind me of a verse in the *Bhagavad Gita*." Then he quoted the Sanskrit sloka from the fifth chapter, verses 8-9.

Naiva kimcit karōmīti
yuktō manyeta tattva-vit
paśyan śṛnvan spṛśan jighrann
aśnan gacchan śvasan svapan
Pralapan visṛjan gṛhnann
unmiṣan nimiṣann api
indriyānīndriyārtheṣu
vartante iti dhārayan

The sage, centered in the Self, realizes, "I do nothing at all." Though seeing, hearing, touching, smelling, eating, walking, emptying, sleeping, holding, opening and closing the eyes, he is assured that only the senses are occupied with their objects.

Amma continued, "Let's see now. where were we? Yes, the saint can go out and return at any time. If he wants to, he will look and see; if he doesn't want to do so, he will remain within his own Self. With the entire universe revolving within him, is anything impossible for him?

"Listen to this story. A woodcutter was chopping wood when a man came up to him, 'Excuse me, but a great procession has just passed by. Can you tell me which way it went?' The woodcutter looked at the man and said, 'I did not even see a procession,' and immediately he went back to his work. Such is the state of the Mahatma. His mind is still. He does not see or hear anything. At the same time, if he wants to, he can let the world in. He can see or hear whatever he wants to, and then he can go within again.

He is both here in the world and there in the Ultimate. But the world cannot touch him. He cannot be deluded or blemished by the world. Although he does everything, he remains untouched."

This raised another question, "How does he do that? How is it possible for him to come and go from the Ultimate at will?"

Mother answered, "When the yogi turns off his mind, the play, or the program, ends. It's just like turning off a television set. When you want to see the program, you press the 'on' button. If you want to watch it, it is there; and when you don't want to watch anymore, you turn the TV off and the program disappears. The on and off button of the mind is in the yogi's hand, under his perfect control.

"If you have something and you can let go of it anytime you want, what does that mean? It means you are not attached to it. You do not possess it and it doesn't bind you. Whether you have it or not, you don't care. This is detachment. Like this, the yogi is in a supreme state of detachment.

"The yogi himself is like a screen. A screen neither projects the play nor does it enjoy it. It is simply the underlying base on which the action of the play takes place. It simply is.

"You may have heard of the great sage, Veda Vyasa. Once he was sitting in samadhi on the banks of the river Yamuna. The gopis of Vrindavan wanted to cross to the other shore, but they couldn't because the river was flooded. It was getting dark, and nowhere could they find a way to cross the river. Finally they saw the sage sitting in meditation. With great hope they approached him. Offering some fruits and flowers at his feet, the gopis prayed to him to help them cross the river. Veda Vyasa awoke from his samadhi. He was pleased, for he knew they were great devotees. Accepting their offerings, he ate everything.

"When he had finished eating the fruits, Vyasa, taking pity on the gopis, raised his hand and said, "If it is true that I have not eaten any of these fruits, let the waters of the Yamuna part and give way to these devout gopis." Lo and behold! The waters parted and the gopis were able to reach the other shore. This is exactly what Mother was speaking about. Though he ate, the sage Vyasa didn't eat anything, and the parting of the river attested to that. Though he caused the waters of the Yamuna to part, he did not do anything because he was in the supreme state of detachment.

"Because you see the saint eating, sleeping, and speaking, you may say that he eats, sleeps and speaks. This is your mind projecting such actions onto him because you yourself eat, sleep and speak. You see only the external. You see only his body, and you think you understand him. Furthermore, you see everybody else doing the same as you, so you think that the yogi is not any different from you. Your own thoughts and actions are projected onto him, yet what you perceive has nothing to do with him. His thoughts and actions are not remotely like yours. You are not familiar with detachment; you know only about attachment, anger, hatred, jealousy, and other negative traits. You therefore project the same familiar traits onto the sage as well. You interpret what he is, and what he does, according to your vasanas.

"Children, have you heard this story? There was once a king who had two great painters in his court. Because a great rivalry existed between them, the king decided to hold a competition. He called them saying, 'We will have a contest to decide who is the better painter. Each of you is to submit a painting using "peace" as the theme.' The first painter chose to paint a still lake in the mountains, with not even a ripple on the surface. Just looking at the lake made the mind still.

"The other artist painted a thundering waterfall full of white foam. Right next to the waterfall was a small bush on which was perched a delicate little bird with its eyes closed. The latter is an example of dynamic silence, silence that can exist in the midst of the busy world. This is the great state of the yogi. He can live peacefully even in the midst of chaos and strife. He remains silent and unaffected, for he is absorbed in deep meditation. Even while living in the problematic world of diversity, the sage is in meditation."

"This state of Oneness is so inexplicable that great souls throughout the ages have found it difficult to describe in words," remarked one devotee.

"Son, you are right, said Amma. "It is such a difficult task because the experience of the Truth is so full, so overflowing and so perfect that words cannot contain it. The intellect cannot grasp it. Even many ordinary, subjective experiences cannot be explained verbally; therefore, how can one possibly talk about the ultimate experience of Truth? This is one of the reasons why many of the scriptures are written in the form of sutras or aphorisms.

"The rishis did not want to talk much. It seems that they wanted to use very few words to describe their experiences. Even they must have found it difficult to put their experiences into words, and thus they felt that sutras would serve as the best mode of expression. They may have anticipated that in the future scholars would interpret and elaborate on what they had written. They probably knew that each scholar would come up with his own interpretation, that each one would invent many different explanations that the rishis themselves had never even dreamt of. They may have surmised that even if they did elaborate on their own experiences, people would still not be content and would instead elaborate on the rishis' elaborations, giving yet further interpretations. Perhaps it was for this reason that they decided to say very little.

"As we can see, this is exactly what has happened. So many commentaries and interpretations now exist on the *Bhagavad Gita* and other scriptural texts. People have been writing, writing, and writing about spirituality for centuries. They can't stop. People's heads are so full of stuff that they want to write, talk, interpret, expound and dispute. Eventually they themselves become confused, and in their confusion they make others confused as well."

Everybody laughed. The last of the visiting devotees were having Mother's darshan. Since there were not many visitors that day, each of the brahmacharis and the other residents of the Ashram also went up to Amma to receive Her blessing. It was a slow and sweet darshan, during which She gave a lot of attention to each devotee.

As the darshan was drawing to an end, the brahmacharis sang one last song

Mauna ghanamritam

The Abode of Dense Silence,
Eternal Peace and Beauty
In which was dissolved the mind of Gautama Buddha,
The Effulgence destroying bondage
The Shore of Bliss beyond the reach of thought
Knowledge that bestows
Perennial equanimity of mind
The Abode having no beginning and no end
Bliss experienced after the movements of mind are hushed
The Seat of Power, Region of Dense Consciousness

The Goal indicated by the statement:
'Thou art That,'
Which grants the sweet eternal Non-dual State
There it is I long to reach
No other ways are there than through Your Grace.

It was nearly two o'clock and nobody had yet had lunch. Getting up from Her cot, Amma called a few of the brahmacharis and asked them to arrange to serve food to the devotees in the dining hall.

She said, "Children, all of you must have lunch prasad before you leave the Ashram." She then looked around as if searching for something. Not finding what She was looking for, Amma asked Gayatri, who was waiting for Amma outside, "Do you have any plantains upstairs? If there are any, bring them." Gayatri went up and returned with some bananas which Mother divided and fed to each devotee. Making sure that everyone received a piece, Amma asked, "Children, did everyone get prasad?"

There was no immediate reply, but after some time a devotee said in a soft voice, "It appears that everybody has, Amma, but we are always happy to get more prasad from your hands. This is a such a rare opportunity."

Amma went up to him and lovingly pinched his ear as a mother does to a mischievous child. Facing all Her children as She bowed, Amma left the darshan hut, followed by Gayatri, and went directly to Her room. The devotees, their hearts full of bliss and contentment, moved to the dining hall to have lunch.

Chapter 4

At five o'clock Mother again came down from Her upstairs room. It was drizzling, so Gayatri held an umbrella over Mother's head. However, Mother did not remain under the umbrella for long because She was walking very quickly. Gayatri followed Mother, trying again and again, without much luck, to protect Her from the rain. Finally, Mother turned around and said to her, "Amma doesn't want the umbrella. She is not going to get a cold or fever. Amma is used to it, so you can have it."

Then She looked back toward the others, including Gayatri, saying to them as they followed, "Children, don't let the rain fall on your head. You might catch cold."

By now all the residents of the Ashram were with Amma as She walked past the kitchen to the bathrooms and toilets. Amma looked into each bathroom and toilet. Because of the heavy rain nobody had paid much attention to them, so they were not very clean. Without uttering a word, Amma entered one of the bathrooms and started cleaning it with a broom and a bucket of water. Everyone who was nearby started running about, trying to find other brooms and buckets with which to clean the remaining bathrooms and toilets. Already they knew that this was going to be a difficult time for them. They knew they were being taught a hard lesson.

Buckets and brooms were soon found, but just as someone was about to enter a bathroom, they all heard Mother's voice,

"No, no. This is not your job. Your job is to meditate, to pray and to study. You are not supposed to do this kind of dirty work. Mother will do this. She is used to doing dirty work. Children, you all come from good families; you should not do this. This is not like meditating and praying. This is different. You should not do anything that you feel is different from meditation; you have all bathed and are ready for the evening bhajan, so not make your bodies stink. Go and meditate!"

Her words were full of sarcasm. Everybody turned pale and stood motionless as if frozen by the impact of Mother's words. Some held brooms in their hands while others had buckets. Nobody dared to enter the bathrooms. They simply could not because of what Mother had said. The message that was hidden in Mother's words had penetrated deeply into each one's heart. They all stood quietly, buckets and brooms in hand, with their heads hanging in shame. Amma cleaned all the bathrooms and toilets by Herself. It was quite a sight to see the Ashram residents standing, holding buckets and brooms in their hands like immovable statues. Had this been a different occasion, watching them would have been a good joke.

After finishing the work, Amma put the broom and the bucket where they were usually kept and without saying another word, She left. Gayatri sincerely wished to follow Her but was afraid to do so. It was still drizzling as Amma went to the edge of the Ashram compound where She lay down on the wet sand. Soon the drizzle turned into rain, as if the rain clouds had been waiting for Mother to lie down. Each resident wanted to fall at Her feet to seek forgiveness. Each one wanted to run to Her and beg Her not to punish Herself because of his negligence, but nobody had the courage to do so.

The rain poured heavily as Mother continued lying in the sand. She was completely drenched. The residents stood at a distance until finally one of them could not control himself any longer. He ran over to Her, calling, "Amma!" Each person had been waiting for this, for somebody to take the initiative. Now, the entire group ran to where Mother was lying. The call, "Amma!" rang through the air like the chorus in a great drama. Everyone was crying, seeking Mother's forgiveness for the mistake. But Mother was not there. She was far beyond the realm of sound and speech. A few moments passed before they realized that Mother was in deep samadhi.

Though Mother most often went into samadhi during bhajans or darshan, apparently from the bliss of devotion, there were also times when Her samadhi states were triggered by some sort of trouble or upset, by incidents involving the negligent or inappropriate behavior of Her children. For no apparent reason these samadhi states lasted longer than the other ones. Once in 1979 Mother entered her family temple and did not come out for a whole day. She remained there for many hours in a completely motionless state. She didn't move or blink, there was no sign of breathing. This came about as the result of a quarrel between Mother's two younger brothers. Mother had tried to intervene, but they would not stop. Mother pleaded and begged, but still they continued to quarrel until their verbal duel became uncontrollable. At this point, Mother rushed into the temple and moving toward one corner became absorbed in deep samadhi.

Because this seemed like a similar type of samadhi, everyone grew worried. Some started crying and praying and some of the brahmacharis began to chant. All the while the rain continued to pour. Umbrellas were brought, but they did not really protect Mother from the fierce pounding of the rain. More than fifteen minutes passed. There was not even a slight movement in Amma's body. Fear and anxiety gripped everyone's heart. Was Mother going to come back from samadhi? Was the pouring rain causing harm to Her body? Everybody was completely drenched by the heavy rain. Finally, it was decided to take Amma to Her room. Assisted by some other women, Gayatri carried Amma up the stairs and into the room while a few brahmacharis continued to chant.

After changing Mother's wet clothes and drying Her, Gayatri, Kunjumol, and some of the women residents massaged Her. A few brahmacharis entered the room and continued chanting. With great emotion, Br. Pai sang a few Sanskrit hymns written by Sankaracharya

> *O Mother, You have many worthy sons on earth,*
> *But among them, I am the most insignificant,*
> *Yet, O Consort of Shiva, it does not befit you*
> *to forsake me,*
> *For now and then a bad son may be born,*
> *But there can never be a bad mother.*

> *There is no sinner like me,*
> *Nor a destroyer of sins like You.*
> *O Mahadevi, knowing all this,*
> *do as You see fit.*

The state of samadhi continued for nearly two hours. A brahmachari had been instructed by Amma about what to do during Her samadhi states. Every now and then he felt the soles of Amma's feet. He did not disclose exactly what the instructions had been, but he said, "Amma once told me that we must be very careful if Her samadhi should continue for more than half an hour. She strictly said that we should sing the Divine Name or chant mantras continuously until She returns to Her normal state."

Around seven-thirty in the evening, Mother returned to the earthly plane of awareness. She remained on the bed, Her eyes transfixed. Gayatri, Kunjumol, and the other women were still massaging Her body. The sound of evening bhajans emerged from the temple verandah, and Mother opened Her eyes. It did not look as if She had yet fully returned from Her transcendent state. The brahmacharis in the room stopped chanting. With a sign of Her hands, Amma asked everyone to leave the room and everyone, except Kunjumol and Gayatri, went out, closing the door behind them. Still concerned about Amma, a few of the brahmacharis wanted to sit in front of Mother's room, but the others felt that nobody should remain there, that if a need arose, either Gayatri or Kunjumol would fetch someone. So they all went down the stairs.

The rain had stopped just a few minutes after Amma was carried in, and shortly afterward, the sky was clear. The fact that the storm arrived so suddenly just as Amma lay down in the sand, and left just as abruptly when She was taken to Her room, made the whole drama look like an act of Divine Will. While only Mother can comprehend the vastness of divine power, to the residents who had been there the storm somehow seemed intimately connected to the lesson Mother was teaching them.

The beauty of work through love

Tuesday, 10 July, 1984

After breakfast, at about ten o'clock, Amma called all the brahmacharis. One by one they came to Amma's room. The brahmacharinis, Gayatri, Kunjumol and Saumya, were also called. When they had all come in, Amma asked one of them to lock the door. When that was done, Amma closed Her eyes, joined Her palms together and sat in a prayerful mood. The brahmacharis all gazed at Her face. Tears streamed down Mother's cheeks. Opening Her eyes for a moment, Amma wiped the tears with a towel and once again closed Her eyes. Suddenly She began to sing

Vedanta venalilude

Where is the truth of the Gita
which proclaims that You will help
A lonely traveller towards Brahman?

Though I am making my way
Through a forestlike path,
for the attainment of You,
And for the peace of my soul,
My mind is filled with sorrow.

O Friend of the miserable,
My heart forever burns for something,
I know not what.
Do You not intend
To remove my sorrow?

O Mother, O Bhagavati Devi,
Do You not know that without merging
Into Your mind-enchanting Being
There is no peace?

This was not simply a devotional song. Amma's heartfelt expressions overflowed through the song, charging the whole atmosphere with a feeling of intense longing. The brahmacharis' eyes also filled with tears as love and devotion permeated the entire room. Amma's radiant face and the way She poured Herself totally into the song touched everyone deeply, creating an indelible memory in the secret chamber of each one's heart.

After the song, there was a deep, profound silence. Amma remained in a meditative mood, and everybody responded by slipping into spontaneous meditation. The meditation continued until everyone was brought back by Mother's favorite mantra, Om Namah Shivaya.

Unexpectedly Amma asked, "Did Mother make Her children sad?" She was referring to the bathroom incident followed by the samadhi state the previous day.

"We must receive such hard lessons, otherwise there is no hope for us," responded a brahmachari.

"Do not think that Amma wanted to frighten you all. It just happened that way. Sometimes it becomes uncontrollable. What to do about this crazy one!"

"We were all very concerned about your body. Why do you have to torture your body because of our mistakes?" said another brahmachari.

Mother's replied, "Those are blissful moments, not torture at all. Amma wanted to be in the rain. Nevertheless, when Her children are very careless, when She sees their lack of shraddha, Amma feels sad. Such sadness sometimes leads Her into a state of absorption. She then feels like withdrawing from the external world. It is when we look on the outside that we see all these faults, lack of alertness and shortcomings. Then She thinks of withdrawing Her mind from this world, this world of events. The very thought of withdrawal is enough, for then She shoots up in no time. The thought that the world and the body are the cause of all those troubles makes Amma close Her eyes to both.

"Children, Amma's body is maintained only for the sake of Her children, and for the world. You should always be aware of this truth. You should remember that to keep this body in the world is not an easy thing. At any time, Amma can put an end to this body's mundane existence. It is Her children's sincerity and steadfast intention on the goal that keeps the body here. It is the call of thousands of sincere seekers and devotees all over the world that draws the body to keep itself down on this plane of existence. Without this, there is no downward pull. This body has no other purpose to be here. Food and sleep are not at all a problem for Amma. She has nothing to do with worldly matters or with wealth. Amma has trained Herself well enough to overcome any situation, adverse or favorable.

"Children, this Ashram is not Amma's. This place exists for the world. It belongs to you, and to all the people who come here. Mother, in fact, has no interest in establishing ashrams or other institutions. She would not have done any of these things if it were not for the world. Amma does these things to help the world. The world should not be filled with selfish people. There should be a few places where at least a handful of people can work and serve selflessly. The beauty and charm of selfless love and service should not die away from the face of this earth. The world should know that a life of dedication is possible, that a life inspired by love and service to humanity is possible.

"Children, Amma expects you to be loving, selfless and very alert in performing your duties. When your heart is filled with love and selflessness, it overflows and expresses itself in all your thoughts, words, and actions. Amma knows that you have not yet attained the state of perfection. But isn't that your goal? You want to live and serve in love, don't you? So you need practice; you must make a constant effort. Amma is very happy if you at least make an attempt to do this. But Mother is very sad when She sees Her children's indolence. Children, never become negligent or sink into apathy. Apathy is the worst state of mind for a spiritual seeker. Someone who is inert is not enthusiastic or interested in anything; he has lost all hope and is bored with life. Such a person is too lazy even to try to get out of his dullness and he becomes a burden to others. His burdensome nature causes anger and hatred to rise within him. His anger forces him to hate everything—his own people, society, God and even his own existence.

"Children, it is necessary to work as we live. Life is precious; therefore, do not waste it by doing things mechanically without love. We should try to put love into everything we do. Machines can do many of the things we do, sometimes even better and more efficiently, but nobody is inspired by a machine. Even though machines can produce greater quantities of work than humans, the quality of love is absent in machine-made products. When love is absent in any action, the action becomes mechanical. People who work mechanically without love become like machines within; they become less human. Humans can love; they can express love and they can live in love—they can even become love."

Amma stopped abruptly. There was silence for a few moments. The clock struck once. It was ten-thirty in the morning. Time itself was warning each soul: "I cannot wait for you; I cannot come back. Whatever you want to do, do it now; do not postpone. I am carrying you toward death, even without your knowledge." Amma was in an absorbed mood. She rocked back and forth with Her eyes closed.

Returning to a normal mood, Amma continued to speak: "There are painters who paint hundreds of thousands of pictures. But there is no depth in their paintings. Nobody feels any attraction to them. They do not penetrate anybody's heart. They do not create any feeling of love or beauty in the viewer's mind. There are many such painters, and they go on painting until they die, but nobody feels inspired by their work.

"There are other painters, however, who do not paint many pictures, maybe just a few. But those few paintings become world famous. People crave to possess one of those paintings. By looking at one of them they feel inspired and amazed. If it is a painting of the ocean, one can feel the vastness and the depth of the sea just by sitting in front of the picture. Just by looking at the painting you are able to experience the sea. You see the waves and you even feel the ocean breeze. Why is this possible? Because of the great love the painter pours into his work. Even if the painting is hung in a matchbox-sized room, it appears to create vast space; the mountains, valleys, rivers and trees become alive. You see beyond the canvas and the paint; you see nature in all its magnificence and glory.

"If a person pours his heart and soul into an activity, it will be transformed into a tremendous source of inspiration. The product of an action performed with love will have a discernible presence of life and light in it. That reality of life and love will make people feel immensely attracted towards it. A Mahatma constantly shows the way. Patiently he instructs you, not once or twice but a thousand times. If you don't listen, if you always disobey, if you still think that you can borrow beauty and love from him instead of working for it yourself, he will withdraw and disappear. A Mahatma has no obligations or duty to the world, other than having created it by their own will, for the good of the world and mankind.

"Children, God has given us the necessary faculties to become like Him. Love, beauty and all divine qualities exist within us. We should make use of our faculties to express these divine qualities in our lives. Don't be lazy and idle away your time. Life is a precious gift. This human body is a rare gift. Work with love while you are still healthy. Do not be a burden to others. God may not have provided you with money, but if you are endowed with a healthy body, work and do it with all your heart.

"Once there was a beggar who was poor but very healthy. He would appeal to anyone who passed by, 'Good people, look at me. God has created me without providing anything. I have nothing, no relatives, nobody to take care of me. Have pity on me.' One day a wise passerby stopped and said to him, 'Okay, give up both your hands to me and I will give you a million dollars.' This caused the beggar to exclaim, 'How can I live without my hands? They are very precious to me!' The wise man then said, 'Okay, don't worry. What about your legs? I offer the same amount for your two legs.' Shocked, the beggar replied, 'Are you crazy? How can I give my legs for a million dollars? My legs are too precious even for that sum." The wise man then asked for the beggar's eyes, but he met with the same response. The beggar said that any part of his body was too precious to be given for a million dollars. The wise man then said to him, 'Look, brother, day after day you are saying that God created you without providing you with anything. Now you yourself have openly declared that your hands, legs and eyes—each part of your body—is very precious to you. Each is priceless you say. So God has certainly given you a precious and priceless body. Why don't you work, using your healthy body to earn a livelihood? Don't just stretch your arms, begging for alms when you are still healthy; that is laziness. God does not like lazy people who want to borrow everything from others. God does not like people who are like parasites; therefore, work, my dear brother, work!'

"Nobody wants to work, to put forth effort to reach the state of perfection. All are eager to know if they can borrow peace, beauty and love from someone or somewhere. When they see the beauty, and love around a Mahatma, they crave it. They want to become like him. They say, 'How beautiful and wonderful you are! I have never experienced so much love and peace in my life. How can I become like you?' So the Mahatma tells them how, but they will not work hard to attain it. Still they want it, so they ask if they can borrow it.

"A Mahatma is the embodiment of the pure love of God, eternal beauty personified. When people meet him, they are attracted to him. Sometimes they too want to become loving and beautiful like him. But when the Mahatma explains to them the ways to attain those qualities, the great renunciation and sur-render that are necessary, they frown and withdraw. They expect to get it free, without doing anything. This body itself is a free gift from God. He gave it simply out of compassion. But human beings are greedy; they always want more. More and more and more—but free! That is their life-long slogan."

"Do your work and perform your duties with all your heart. Try to work selflessly with love. Pour yourself into whatever you do. Then you will experience beauty and love in every field of work. Love and beauty are within you. Try to express them through your actions and you will definitely touch the very source of bliss.

Again there was a pause. Amma moved her right hand in circles while softly chanting, Shiva.... Shiva... Shiva... Shiva... Everybody had been keenly listening to the parable Mother had just related and to the explanation which followed. Amma asked the brahmacharis to sing *Maname nara jivitamakkum*. When they started the song, Amma also joined in

Maname nara jivitamakkum

O mind, this human birth is like a field;
If not cultivated properly
It becomes dry and barren.
You know not how to sow the seeds
Nor how to grow them well,
Neither have you the wish to know.

By removing the weeds and putting fertiliser,
By taking proper care,
You will have a good harvest.

The early part of life
Is spent in helpless cries
And youth is spent in lustful attachment.

As old age approaches
Your strength is taken away,
You become like a helpless worm
Biding your time, with nothing to do
Looking forward only to the grave.

After this song a brahmachari asked, "Amma, your statement that the Mahatma will withdraw and disappear if the disciples don't listen and obey him sounded like a warning to us all. Are you trying to say that you too will do the same if we act indiscriminately?" There was fear and anxiety in his voice.

Amma consoled him, patting his back as She began to speak, "Son, try not to compare. Amma was not saying that She too will go away if you don't listen to Her. Amma was indicating that the Mahatma has nothing to lose or gain. You are the losers if you do not follow his words. You will lose the beauty, love, and peace which you see in him and in his actions. In a way, it is his disappearance from your life, isn't it? Mother was simply trying to express that we should perform our actions with love and dedication. Try to follow the footsteps of the Guru with all your heart. Obedience to the Guru's words is the only way to cross over all obstacles which arise in the spiritual path.

"Amma is saying that love alone lends attraction and beauty to our actions. No work is insignificant or meaningless. The amount of love that you pour into your work makes it significant and beautiful.

"You may think that cleaning the bathroom is dirty work. Try to feel that cleaning the bathroom is an opportunity to serve the devotees who visit the Ashram. If you can, clean a dirty public place without anybody's insistence. Do it just out of concern for others. That action becomes a beautiful piece of work. Your pure attitude beautifies the work. An unknown feeling of joy springs forth within you as a result of doing it.

"Behind all great, unforgettable events lies the heart. Love and a selfless attitude underlie all truly great deeds. Behind any good cause, you will find somebody who has renounced everything and dedicated his or her life to it.

"Look at your mother cooking. She does it with love. Look at a farmer working in the field. The farmer can create waves of beauty in his work if he does it with love and sincerity. You can see that his heart is in his work; you can feel his heart flowing toward it. He is happy and enthusiastic while he tends to his chores. Loudly singing or humming a folk melody, he works tirelessly, without being bothered about food or sleep, or what happens around him. He is patient; he is not worried about the amount of time the work will consume. He enjoys plowing, sowing, irrigating and harvesting by himself. This is the meaning of the word sincerity. Sincerity means the ability to put your whole heart into what you do, the ability to love your work.

"Children, you must do your work with sincerity. Whether you consider it significant or insignificant, whether you like it or not, you should do your work with interest and love. When you work in this way, when love begins to flow into all that you do, your work becomes sadhana. It becomes less and less difficult, until one day all physical and mental exertion are gone. From then on, you will start working with your whole heart. Love blossoms within you and it will be reflected in all that you do.

"Even a saint, after attaining Self-realization, might continue doing the same work he did before, like sweeping the road or working in the fields. But now his attitude is different. After Realization he is totally detached. He is the observer of all that he does. Full of innocence and wonder, the saint never gets bored. He is like a child who never tires of hearing the birds sing, who never gets bored looking at flowers, who is always thrilled by the rising moon. Like a child's world, the saint's life is filled with wonder. For him, everything is new and fresh, because he beholds the essential nature of everything with love."

Amma stopped and said, "There has been a lot of talking. Let us now stop and look within for some time before we close." Amma sang a kirtan to which everybody responded

Chintakalkantyam

O Glorious Light of Eternal Bliss
Dawning within me when my thoughts have ended,
Pondering on Your golden feet
I have happily given up everything.

When You are there as my own,
I need no other relatives.
Give up quickly the ignorance of selfishness!
This mind will not be gloomy any more
As it sheds the flower of desire.
Let it dissolve in Your light and enjoy great peace.

Please dwell within me to help me live like air,
Having contact with everything
Yet having connection with none.
Think, O man! Why are you living?
Do you follow the ways of the animal kingdom?

After the blissful singing, everybody sat in a meditative mood as instructed by Amma. Then Amma took a portion of the lunch which had been brought for Her, and dividing it up into small balls, She began to feed everyone with Her own hands. Each brahmachari approached Amma to receive his share of prasad. While feeding Her children, Amma delighted in telling jokes, rejoicing in the moment with the brahmacharis. One of them who always acted like a little child in front of Amma came twice.

He was caught red-handed. She said loudly, "Look here, here is a thief. He already came once and got his share." The brahmachari innocently replied, "Give me one more. Then I'll come only one more time." Everybody burst into laughter. Amma too laughed heartily at this childlike reply of the brahmachari.

Finally Gayatri's turn came. Amma took a ball of rice and was about to feed her. Gayatri sat with her mouth wide open, ready to receive the prasad, but suddenly Amma withdrew Her hand. Once again laughter filled the air. Gayatri flushed with slight embarrassment. Then Amma said, "Here, my darling daughter, take it." Again she opened her mouth as Amma brought the ball of rice closer to her, almost touching her lips. Again at the last moment, Amma pulled back, as another roar of laughter filled the room. When it subsided, Amma looked mischievously at Gayatri, whose face was flushed with embarrassment, then gently but deliberately popped the rice ball into her mouth. Hugging her most affectionately, Amma kissed Gayatri on both cheeks.

It was a very touching scene. An indescribable expression of love and compassion shone on Amma's face. Feeling the qualities of motherhood overflowing, some brahmacharis found it hard to withhold their tears.

Because Gayatri constantly lives with Her, Amma stresses that Gayatri should be perfect in every way. Amma would say, "Gayatri-mol should be like a second mother for everyone, so much so that Amma does not spare her, not even for the smallest mistake." Amma's love and compassion for Gayatri are indescribable. Rare are the occasions when they are expressed, but when they are, it is always a heart-gladdening sight. This was one such occasion.

Being fed by Amma was always a treat for Her children. At one time the affectionate ritual occurred almost daily. But as the number of residents increased, it became more and more unusual. There was also something else which caused it to stop.

In the early days, before there was a strict Ashram routine, Nealu, Gayatri, Unni and Balu were the only resident disciples. The other brahmacharis, who were still working or studying, used to visit the Ashram frequently, for circumstances were such that they could not be permanent residents. Whenever these brahmacharis came to visit, whether together or alone, Amma used to feed them. She also used to feed all the devotees who were present during lunch. Even after the first group of brahmacharis came to stay permanently, Amma continued the habit of feeding each person.

Later, however, when the brahmacharis started learning the scriptures, they were taught to chant before each meal. They chanted the fifteenth chapter of the Srimad Bhagavad Gita, followed by Brahmarpanam from the fourth chapter, verse 24

Brahmārpanam brahma havir
brahmāgnaubrahmanā hutam
brahmaiva tena gantavyam
brahma-karma-samādhinā

The oblation is Brahman,
the ghee is Brahman,
offered by Brahman in the fire of Brahman;
unto Brahman verily he goes
who cognizes Brahman alone in his actions.

Thus, one day Amma announced, "Now that you are chanting this mantra, Amma will not feed you every day as She used to do. From this day on, do not expect it. The mantra must be practiced. If everything is Brahman, you too are Brahman. How can Brahman be fed?"

From that day on, the daily practice of feeding stopped. Yet, to this day Amma still feeds Her Ashram children, but only once in a while. Still, it is a special experience, one that cannot be put into words. It is not merely rice or some other food that She gives. Rather, into this prasad Amma transmits Her love, purity, compassion, and concern for Her children.

Chapter 5

At about four-thirty in the afternoon Amma was playing with some children from the neighboring houses, some of whom were children of devotees. She made a temple for them with wet sticky sand. Using flowers and leaves She decorated the roof. When the temple was completed, a consecration ceremony was performed, and Amma installed a small picture of Krishna inside the temple of sand. Amma was totally lost in this play, and the children were very happy. When the ceremony was over, they all stood up as instructed by Amma and began to circumambulate the temple. Amma led the singing of *Agatanayai* with the children singing the response.

Agatanayai

Lord Vishnu has come!
Lord Vishnu has come!
Let us always offer worship to the Lord.
The Supreme Lord of the world has come,
Giving comfort to the world.

The Lord has come to the earth
To rid the men of earth of sorrow.

Has the Lord of Peace, full of compassion,
Descended to show the way to Liberation?

It did not look as if they were playing at all as Mother and the children sang and rejoiced, clapping their hands. On the contrary, the whole scene had the appearance of a genuine event. After circling the temple for some time, Amma and the children began to dance to the tune of Krishna... Krishna, Radha... Krishna. Closing their eyes like Amma, they all danced for some time with great enthusiasm and glee. After this song Amma sat down and meditated, and the children followed Her example. Each child sat in perfect posture and meditated until Amma called and gently shook them one by one, telling them to get ready for the distribution of prasad. Amma had already put some toffees in front of the temple which were now distributed as prasad to the children.

It was such a lovely and inspiring sight. The residents of the Ashram who were watching from a distance sincerely wished that they were children so that they too could join Amma. Some of them began to move closer to watch, but others prevented them from doing so. They thought that their presence might spoil the beauty of Mother's time with these little children; therefore, they all watched Amma's play from a distance.

The children did not want to leave Amma, who played with them just like another child of their age. They continued to sit around Her and they were having a lot of fun talking, laughing and cracking jokes. They were really celebrating; a real festival was taking place. Hearts were overflowing and being expressed as blissful laughter.

After having played with the children for another half an hour, Amma got up and walked toward the temple. The beautiful notes from Br. Sreekumar's flute emerged from one of the huts and filled the atmosphere. Still surrounded by the children, Amma came and stood in front of the temple. One of the girls, who was about six or seven years old, begged: "Ammachi, let's sing and play the game of temple again." She caught hold of Amma's hand and asked again and again.

Turning toward the little girl and affectionately stroking her cheeks, Amma said, "Child, that is enough for today. Amma has many other things to do."

"I liked the play very much," said the little girl. "Can we do it again tomorrow?"

Extremely pleased with the child and her innocence, Amma gave her a big hug and kissed her on both cheeks, repeating, "Darling daughter... Amma's darling daughter."

Releasing the girl from Her arms, Amma asked her, "Will you always be devoted like this, even when you grow up?"

The girl nodded her head affirmatively.

While being in the midst of children, Mother also becomes like a child, playing and frolicking with them. Amma makes them feel that She is one of them. Amma always gives a special place to children, and they feel it. Anyone who has watched Her with young children knows this to be true. The children are given so much attention. Amma makes them feel comfortable and happy as She holds them on Her lap. Seating them next to Her, She carefully and attentively listens to their prattles or complaints. They have their own place and significance in Amma's presence. They feel this so clearly that some children do not want to leave Her, not even when the rest of their family is ready to go. Many children have more love for Amma than for their own fathers and mothers. This attachment children have toward Amma arises from the pure love and genuine concern She shows them. Children are so receptive that Amma's Divine Love penetrates directly into their hearts. With such easy access, Amma touches them deeply and they feel it immediately. Pure, unconditional love is the secret behind all this.

Discrimination

Amma sat in the front yard of the temple on the sand and was soon surrounded by the residents. Just then, Harshan, Amma's cousin, came to the spot where She and the others were sitting. He was lame and walked with a limp. Harshan had great devotion for Amma. Even when the entire family had stood against Her, Harshan strongly supported Amma and had great sympathy for Her. Just to make Amma laugh, he used to act in funny ways sometimes. He prostrated and sat with the others. Amma was very pleased to see him. He was working on a fishing boat, so Amma inquired about his work. As it was the rainy season, Mother wanted to know about the general well-being of the fishermen. A short chat followed about how the monsoon had badly affected the fisherfolk.

Harshan had a peculiar way of singing devotional songs, gesturing with his hands and making various facial expressions. Amma asked him to sing a kirtan. Without a moment's hesitation he began to sing; sometimes he stretched his hands out toward Mother, at other times he gestured like a professional musician with one hand on his chest and the other raised high. His facial expressions were sometimes exaggerated and other times he closed his eyes, and with palms joined, bowed reverently to Mother. The song was

Sundarini vayo

Please come, O Beautiful One
Consort of Shiva, please come
O Auspicious One, please come
Please come, O Endless One.

O Vamakshi, Consort of Lord Shiva
O Kamakshi who radiates brilliance everywhere

To those who look upon You
As their Dear Relation, You are their very own.

O Mother, please remain
As the spring of my inspiration.
Being both of one and of many forms,
You are the Light of the Absolute.

Do You not know my heart well?
Will You not come before me
Even now as I ask?

Amma looked very happy while listening to the song, but sometimes She laughed like an innocent child seeing his gestures. As he finished the song, he knelt and bowed to Her. Mother lovingly gave him a strong pat on his back, and Harshan playfully fell down to one side. This aroused thunderous laughter. Mother too laughed loudly.

The light playful scene created by Harshan was transformed by a profound teaching of Amma when She answered a question asked by a brahmachari: "Amma, I have heard you say that a spiritual seeker transcends everything once he attains the state of Perfection. Does that mean that he also goes beyond discrimination, which is considered an important quality that a competent seeker should have?"

Amma's answer was illuminating, "Children, discrimination is meant for one who is in the process of evolution. You need strict discrimination to understand the difference between what is good for your spiritual progress and what will create obstacles in your path. A seeker must discriminate between what is eternal and what is non-eternal. But once you have attained the state of Perfection, you have renounced everything, even discrimination. You cannot hold onto anything. Transcending all dualities, you become the universe; you become expansiveness itself. You become both day and night. You go beyond purity and impurity.

"In the Thousand Names of the Divine Mother, the Lalita Sahasranama, are the mantras *Sad-asad-rupa dharini*—one who takes the forms of both being and nonbeing, and *Vidyavidya svarupini*—one who is both knowledge and ignorance. These verses mean that Devi, Pure Consciousness, is everything and beyond everything. If consciousness is everywhere and all-pervading, then everything that is is consciousness only.

"But you should always remember that this statement about the Absolute is not suitable for seekers, those who are still striving to reach the goal. This is not applicable to them at all. Amma is talking about the state of Absolute Consciousness. Nothing is without consciousness for one who is fully established in Reality. Everything is pervaded with consciousness and therefore, there are no differences. When everything is pervaded with consciousness, how can there be any discrimination? A Perfect Soul has no mind, no ego. He has no vasanas, not even in their unmanifested state, for he has completely uprooted them. His mind has become permanently silent and still forever and ever.

"Children, the do's and don'ts, what is pure or impure, good or bad, are only for ordinary people. A Mahatma, who is beyond body consciousness, is not affected by such rules. He is completely untouched. But if a Mahatma chooses to remain in the world for the uplifting of society, he will observe the rules of society. He will strictly follow them in order to set an example for others. The world needs that. People need morality, good character, and purity to be able to evolve.

"Ordinary people still have body-consciousness; therefore, they cannot act like evolved souls who are beyond all standards of behavior. Without rules of conduct an ordinary person's life would be a disaster. A sadhak too must have a disciplined life;

otherwise, he cannot progress. He cannot imitate a Great Soul who is established in the state of the beyond. The sadhak should sincerely try to follow the Mahatma's or the Guru's instructions, but he should not try to imitate the Mahatma or the Guru.

"Children, Amma used to live only on water and tulasi leaves. She even used to forgo food and sleep for several months at a time. There was a time when Amma ate raw fish, used tea leaves, pieces of glass and sometimes dirt. She never felt that any of those things were dirty or impure. At that time, there was neither love nor any lack of love. There was neither compassion nor any lack of compassion. What there was was just like space or the sky—an endless expansiveness. Amma was totally absorbed in that non-dual state and never wanted to return.

"How can there be any concept of purity or impurity, dirty or clean, ugly or beautiful in space? How can there be any thought of discrimination in the state of expansiveness, where there are no thoughts and no mind? That state contains everything; it accommodates everything. In fact, both good and bad exist in that space. It is like the river carrying everything within it and washing everything away. The river doesn't discriminate. It cannot say, "Only healthy people can bathe in me. I won't let beggars and lepers wash in my waters." The river Ganges cannot say that. She caresses everything and carries everything, both good and bad. She accepts even dead and rotting bodies into her flow.

"But then for Amma this state changed. The call from within transformed everything. Once you make a sankalpa to be in the body and to work to save the world, the circumstances become such that you have to follow the traditional ways of society's rules of conduct. Otherwise, if social norms are ignored, society is disrupted. If you behave in a strange way without following the moral and traditional norms, you will do harm to other people around you; you will be destroying rather than saving the world.

"All names and forms are divisions created by the mind. He who has attained the state of perfection transcends the mind and intellect. For him names and forms drop away. He becomes space; he becomes expansiveness. He may be carrying a body around, and yet, he really doesn't carry it. He just does what he does, just eats what he eats, just says what he says. He simply is. He exists in an undifferentiated state. He is not bothered by the world, nor does he bother about the world or its uplift. Amma is talking about that Supreme State where there is no mind or thought. Do not fail to understand that this is about the experience of that Supreme State. It is easy to misunderstand, for you can keep on talking about the highest state, and yet you won't understand anything.

"Remember, there are some enlightened beings who are ready to sacrifice themselves to the world. They are the ones who choose to participate in the world and lead seekers and devotees to God, by setting an example through their words and deeds. Once they decide to remain in the body for the transformation of society, they dwell in the highest state of discrimination. This discrimination is the constant experience that Brahman alone is real and that the world (*jagat*), is unreal. Internally they constantly dwell in that supreme state, but outwardly they tirelessly and selflessly work for the good of the world, observing all the moral norms of society. Again, remember that this is only when you remain in the body after Realization. Otherwise, you are what you are. But for a sadhak who is still striving to reach the state of Perfection, discrimination between good and bad, between the eternal and the non-eternal, is absolutely necessary."

Compassion makes a mahatma take a body

Knowing that Mother was speaking from experience, a brahmachari inquired, "Amma, you said that you too were in a totally absorbed state for some time. What made you come down from that supreme state?"

"Compassion," came Her reply. "Somehow, a thought arose. No, not somehow; it was simply there. The idea to be compassionate was always there. That was the sankalpa. By holding onto that thought of compassion, Amma could return to this world.

"Compassion is the quality which keeps this body here in the world. If that sankalpa of compassion were not there, the Mahatma would not return to the world but would remain in that state of absorption. His behavior may seem strange, and he may be misunderstood. People have preconceived ideas even about a Self-Realized soul, who dwells in a state where no ideas can reach. They try to fit him in the cage of their limited ideas. A Mahatma cannot be stereotyped; therefore, they will call him crazy.

"You may have heard of the saint named Naranattu Bhrantan, who lived in Kerala a few hundred years ago. He was an *avadhuta*,[3] well-known for his strange personality and behavior. Once a seeker wanted to become his disciple and follow him wherever he went. The man approached the saint and expressed his wish, but the Mahatma was not willing to accept anybody as his disciple and immediately denied the man's request. Nevertheless, the man was very insistent, and finally the saint agreed to his request. "You may follow me,' he said, 'but under one condition. Whatever I do, you too must do exactly the same.' 'That should be easy,' the man said with enthusiasm, and off he went with the saint.

"Naranattu Bhrantan walked and walked and walked. He never rested. He did not eat or drink for several days. He didn't sleep or talk. The man soon became exhausted. He tried to keep pace with the Mahatma, but he could not go on much longer. At last he told the saint, 'I will die if I do not eat or drink something soon.' Not long after that they came to a blacksmith's workshop

---

[3] A Self-realized soul who has transcended all social conventions.

where lead was being melted. The Mahatma walked up to the pot of boiling lead and started drinking the lead using his bare cupped hands.

Turning to his friend, he said, 'Hey, come here! Drink as much as you want.' The man stepped back, turned around and ran away as fast as his legs could carry him. The saint in the story was known as a bhrantan which means 'the crazy one.' Because they did not understand him, people thought he was mad. He accepted this and never tried to correct them or to teach them. He never tried to make them understand the meaning of his actions. He was never bothered by the world or by what they thought of him."

"Children, there is another interesting story about him. Naranattu Bhrantan used to cook his food in graveyards, using the funeral pyre as fuel. It is said that one night while he was cooking, a demigoddess who dances around funeral pyres appeared. She and her retinue came to perform their midnight ritual dance. She ordered Bhrantan to leave the graveyard immediately because she could not dance in the presence of humans. The Mahatma was not about to budge so a huge dispute ensued between the two. She let out a roar and said that it was her nightly routine to dance around the funeral pyre and that under no circumstances would She break her regular routine. The Mahatma smiled and said coolly, 'If you are so strict about your regular routine, so am I. It is my daily routine to cook food over a funeral pyre in a graveyard; therefore, I cannot leave. If you are so insistent upon dancing, why don't you go find some other graveyard? I will not move.'

"Seeing that this man was very determined and stubborn, the demigoddess and her retinue tried to frighten him by roaring loudly and making threatening gestures. The Mahatma just smiled. He remained very calm and unperturbed. Watching the whole scene with childlike innocence, he laughed heartily at their fierce display. Finally, the demigoddess gave up. She realized that the man was not an ordinary soul. She changed her tone: 'O great one, I give up. Let your wish be done. I will leave, but before I go, I would like to grant you a boon. Please ask for one.' The Mahatma replied, 'I don't want any boons. There is nothing I need to achieve, and I have no desires to be fulfilled. My only prayer is to be left alone. Let me concentrate on my cooking.'

"Nonetheless, the demigoddess continued to insist that he ask for a boon, so at last the Mahatma gave in: 'Okay, tell me the exact date of my death.' She told him. Again she requested that he ask for another boon, since the first one was no great favor at all. 'All right,' said the saint. 'Now, can you postpone my death by one day or make it come sooner by one day?' The demigoddess replied that such a thing was beyond her control, so please, wouldn't he ask for something else?

"Taking pity on her, the Mahatma pointed to his left foot which was afflicted with elephantiasis saying, 'Since you are so keen on granting me a boon, transfer this disease from the left foot to the right one.' When that was done, he requested her to leave as he did not want any more boons. In obedience, the demigoddess immediately disappeared from the spot, taking with her all her followers.

"Strange are the ways of a Mahatma. Human intellect cannot understand great souls and, therefore, call them crazy. Their apparent craziness has a purpose which is to make human beings realize their own craziness for name, honor and wealth. Only if humans realize their own craziness can such craziness be removed. A Mahatma has nothing to achieve or gain. He is beyond all achievements. He has attained all that is to be attained and is ever full to the brim. When his heart overflows, that is known as love and compassion. He can remain totally drawn within, and he can also overflow with love if he chooses.

"This story is meant to show the attitude of a completely surrendered soul. The story illustrates how all aspects of divinity are perfectly under a Mahatma's control. There is no fear in him; there is neither anxiety nor excitement. He is not worried or disturbed about anything. Even though he can change destiny or prarabdha if he wishes, he willingly accepts it. He does not want to change it. Fearless as he is, he wants to pass willingly through all experiences. Fear results when people are tossed about by their own petty desires, always concerned only about themselves. Once you overcome fear, you can smile, looking at all the challenges of life. A Mahatma has transcended vasanas by controlling desires and thought waves. That gives him the power to smile heartily, simply looking at everything."

But, did you notice that the Mahatma in this story had no compassion? He had neither compassion nor lack of compassion. He was not at all concerned about the world. He always remained in the Absolute State. He was almost like a bodiless person. Compassion is the quality which makes a Mahatma remain in society and work for its uplifting. It is only out of that quality of compassion that he helps sadhaks, devotees, disciples and anyone who approaches him."

The time for the evening bhajan was approaching. Amma asked everyone to go and get ready. She went and sat in Her usual place in front of the temple. One by one the residents came and took their seats on the temple verandah. Amma remained on Her seat, leaning against the wall. Fixing Her gaze skywards, She was lost to this world.

Soon the verandah was filled with the residents. The singing started even though Amma did not participate in the beginning. She sat motionless, looking beyond this world.

Br. Sreekumar sang *Arikullil,* a song he had composed when he was away from Mother. The song describes his excruciating pain of separation from Amma. Therefore, it was filled with feelings of the heart. The same feelings were expressed as he sang

Arikullil

Setting in the western ocean, the sun
Has marked the close of day in its sad lament.
It is but the play of the Universal Architect,
So why feel dejected, O closing lotuses?

This world so full of misery and deep in sorrow,
Is but the drama of God, the Maker-Creator,
And I am but a marionette, helpless in His hands
No tears have I to shed, as I'm looking on.

Like a flame I'm burning up, separated from You,
Burning and burning is my mind
In this ocean of grief I'm tossed about
Not finding the shore.

After the first song Amma joined in the singing of *Nilambuja*. Her heart overflowed, creating wave after wave of bliss and ecstasy.

Nilambuja

O Mother with blue lotus eyes,
Will You not listen to the sobbing of this sorrowing heart?
Perhaps due to the deeds of some past birth
I am wandering alone.

Through ages and ages have I passed
Before taking birth now.
Will You not take me to You
With a motherly hug and put me on Your lap?

Not deserving I may be
But, O Mother, will You forsake this child for this reason?
Will You not come, take me close
And give me a merciful glance?

Chapter 6

Sunday, 22 July, 1984

At ten-thirty in the morning Amma was already in the hut giving darshan to Her children. Since it was Sunday, a Devi Bhava
day, many people had come to receive the blessings of the Holy
Mother. Even though it rained nearly every day during the monsoon season, devotees did not allow the weather to prevent them
from coming to receive Mother's darshan.

To watch Amma give darshan to Her children is always a
unique experience. The people came and moved one by one before
Her. Some cried and poured their hearts out to Her, seeking blessings and grace, while others laughed and rejoiced, expressing their
happiness and gratitude to Amma for Her infinite grace. There
were some who wanted nothing but to be spiritually uplifted.
They prayed for Her constant guidance and mercy. Some had
desires to be fulfilled and others wanted Amma to solve their
problems. It was an endless chain of people and problems. She
consoled those who wept, wiped their tears, and assured them that
She would be with them always. Amma laughed with those who
rejoiced and whole-heartedly participated in their happiness. No
wonder people braved stormy weather to come to seek comfort
and solace from Amma. Her protective wings spread out as broad
as the universe itself. Reaching far and wide, Amma guarantees
loving care for all Her children.

Be courageous

During the course of the darshan, a young man approached Mother and complained that he had been having terrible neck pain for the last two years. He said that he had been experiencing the agonizing pain day and night. The young man added that he could never sleep soundly because the pain increased tremendously when night fell. Even as he spoke to Mother, the young man looked as if he were experiencing severe pain.

Amma listened to him with a mischievous smile on Her face. This was quite unusual. Usually when somebody approached Her with such a problem, Amma would clearly become identified with the person and his pain. She would sympathize with him, console him, and lovingly rub the affected area. Thus Amma would share the pain in every possible way. However, to this young man Amma did not show any love or compassion. She continued to smile and kept looking at his face for a while. Slowly the smile disappeared and Her face became very serious. Amma looked straight into the young man's eyes. The look and Her eyes were so penetrating that the young man could not face Her; he hung his head. A few moments passed, but the young man did not dare raise his head.

The look on Amma's face became still more serious and then She spoke, "Look here, is this the place to enact your drama?" The voice sounded deep and awesome.

The young man raised his head. He was struck with fear and started trembling. Finally he emitted a loud cry and burst into tears. Through the tears he cried, "Forgive me! Forgive me! Don't curse me. Don't punish me. I am frightened. I tried to pretend that I was suffering from neck pain. Please forgive me... Please forgive me... Please forgive me..." The young man repeated these words over and over again.

Seeing his helpless condition, Amma could not help but allow Her motherly compassion to overflow. "Son, son," She said, "no problem. No problem, don't worry. How can Amma curse you or punish you? She can do neither. How can a mother even dream of doing such a thing? Don't cry. Be relaxed. Be consoled. Do not feel frightened. You were forgiven as soon as you realized your mistake. Don't cry." Amma hugged the young man, wiped his tears, put him on her lap and rubbed his back with great love and compassion.

The young man was an atheist who had no faith at all in Amma. He thought She was just an ordinary village girl to whom people attributed divinity. Armed with an invented story, he had come to expose Her. The young man's plan was to make Amma believe that he had severe neck pain. He expected that She would comfort and soothe him, and only after that would he secretly reveal the truth to Amma. In his dream of pride and success, he had thought he was going to walk proudly out after accomplishing this, but his plan had crumbled. He had intended to humble Mother, but it was he who was humbled instead.

The young man cried and sought forgiveness from Amma. Then, feeling somewhat consoled, he raised his head from Amma's lap and sat down near Mother, his head still hanging. Mother resumed giving darshan to the devotees, and the brahmacharis sang

Amma Amma Taye

O Mother, Mother, dear Divine Mother
Goddess of the Universe
Giver of food to all creatures
You are the Primal Supreme Power.

Everything in the world happens
Because of Your Divine Play.

Protect me, Mother, O Mother, protect me
Without conceiving in the womb
You have given birth
to millions and millions of beings.

You are my life's goal, O Mother
Do not ignore me, O Goddess of the World.
You are the Goddess Lalita, Ruler of the World.

O Mother, if You throw me into trouble
again and again
Who else is there to protect me?
O Mother with enchanting eyes,
You are the Omnipresent Witness of all.

After the song, the young man again began to sob like a child. Amma smilingly glanced at him and said, "Son, don't feel ashamed. Forget about the incident. Be courageous. You were courageous enough to come in front of Amma pretending that you had a terrible neck pain. Where is that great courage now? When you set out to do something, whether it be right or wrong, you should also be daring enough to face whatever consequences it brings you. There are many who have chosen an unrighteous path. They may even be aware that their path is wrong. Still they proceed along their chosen way, determined to confront and overcome whatever results may occur, whether favorable or not.

"But, now look at yourself and the state you're in. Can't you be a little more courageous? Son, either you surrender or declare war. Surrendering needs a little more courage. The one who surrenders to the Supreme Being is the most courageous of all. In fact, the one who declares war is afraid. It is fear that motivates him to declare war. He fears he will lose and the other will win. He fears that his ideas will not survive. He fears that he will not be able to overpower his adversary. The thought of the opponent always disturbs him. Day and night he thinks about the enemy. The opposition creates hell in his mind and thus he lives in constant fear. Ravana, abductor of Sita, was in constant fear of Her husband, Rama. Kamsa, the wicked uncle of Sri Krishna, lived always in fear of his nephew. Duryodhana, the eldest son of the blind King Dhritharasthra, was in constant fear of the Pandavas.

"The atheists of today are of that nature; they live in fear. But unlike the heroes of the old days, the people who boast that they are nonbelievers do not have the courage to bear the consequences of their actions. Those ancient heroes were also skeptics and rationalists, but they were far more courageous than today's skeptics and nonbelievers.

"Yet, in spite of their courage to do unrighteous deeds, they still lived in fear. Ravana was afraid that Rama would destroy him when He came to rescue Sita. The fear that Krishna would come and kill him haunted Kamsa all the time. And Duryodhana was fearful of the power of the Pandavas, especially since Krishna was with the Pandavas. Fear made the lives of these men a living hell. They constantly devised plots and plans to kill their enemies. Never at peace within themselves, they lived with tension and despair. This is what happens to those who are unwilling to surrender.

"Surrender removes all fear and tension. Surrender leads one to peace and bliss. Where there is surrender there is no fear, and vice versa. Where there is surrender there is love and compassion, whereas fear results in hatred and enmity. But to surrender one needs a lot of courage, the courage to give up oneself. It demands a daring attitude to sacrifice one's ego. Surrender means welcoming and accepting everything without the least feeling of sorrow or disappointment.

"Therefore, son, if you want to fight, it is all right. Continue all your efforts to expose Amma as a fraud. At least be daring and determined. Look at you, you have lost your strength and confidence. You mustn't let that happen. Be courageous and don't lose self-confidence."

The young man remained silent. He seemed deep in thought. A few devotees who were sitting nearby expressed their anger toward him with some sharp remarks. Amma stopped them, saying, "No, no. You must not do that. Don't hurt his feelings. By making such rough comments you are setting a bad example. Amma does not want to criticize or abuse him. Amma is telling him these things only for his own point of reference, for his own good. He is free to accept or reject them.

"Besides that, your expression of anger is releasing the negative vasanas within yourselves. Use your discrimination. You must learn how to listen and respond, without reacting. Therefore, children, Amma will not allow you to be mean to him. She does not want you to condemn him. Why should we do that? What good would it do him or you? Condemnation will only spoil your mind as well as his. That is not the right attitude. Reaction will benefit neither your victim nor you. Therefore, don't react. Learn how to respond."

Response as opposed to reaction

One of the devotees who had expressed anger toward the young man asked Amma, "Amma, what do you mean by response? Reaction, of course we always react. But how does one respond?"

Amma explained the difference: "Response can be explained in many different ways. It is total acceptance. It is also non-acceptance with a positive attitude. It can also be neither acceptance nor rejection. You simply remain watching the reaction which arises from you. But you remain apart from it. You don't get involved at all. Remember, you see it, and when you see it, you are not part of it. You are watching it. You are not in the scene. In order to respond, one should become like a mirror. One should become a clear reflector of the others' feelings. A mirror just reflects but never gets involved; it is never touched or tainted by the images.

"It is as if you are watching a movie. You are outside of it. You simply look and observe; you enjoy the play. You enjoy the experience of watching the play; you never become involved in the play or the experience. It is beautiful if you can do this. You can stand apart from what is happening and simply laugh at it. Only a compassionate person can respond.

Out of this explanation, a question arose, "Is it possible for an ordinary person to do this?"

"This kind of doubting will certainly not make it possible," was Amma's reply. "Children, if you want to fulfill a worldly goal, for example, to make a million dollars, you start immediately. You don't waste any time. You can't wait. You strive hard; you work diligently in order to accomplish your goal. You work with enthusiasm. You forget everything else—even food and sleep—in your urgent determination to reach your goal. When you want to become a doctor or an engineer, you study hard to achieve it. But when your goal is something spiritual, something which will really help you to lead a peaceful life, you have a hundred doubts about it, a hundred questions about it's possibility. What a pity! By not even trying, you are defeated before you even begin.

"The human intellect has taken man to great heights in the field of science. There was a time when people believed that many of the things which science has attained today were absolutely impossible. They never even dreamed that human beings could go to the moon or that people, while sitting in their homes looking at a small machine called a TV, could see events occurring in another part of the world. Think of the once unimaginable developments of modern science that are now taken for granted. From where do all these things come? What is behind all these wonderful inventions? They are achievements of the human intellect.

"These achievements are the clear-cut proof of the tremendous power inherent in the human mind which is directed toward scientific discovery. And yet, the power of a scientist's intellect is only an infinitesimal portion of the infinite power inherent in the human mind. The power of the human mind is immeasurable.

"This infinite power is in all human beings. If a person really wants to do something, nothing is impossible for him. Nothing can enslave him, overpower him or control him, if he is courageous enough to dive deep into his own mind, his own consciousness. He can tap into the very source of all power. Amma can guarantee this, provided the efforts are sincere.

"There are many masters around the world who have attained that ultimate state. If they could do it, you too should be able to do it. Why doubt? Try. Doubting is something that you learn to do; you learn to doubt. You never learn to believe. Doubt is your number one enemy. Faith is your best friend. Have faith and make the effort. You will see the outcome."

A group of devotees who had come from the northern part of Kerala started singing verses from the

Devi Mahatmyam

O Devi, You who remove the sufferings of Your supplicants, be gracious. Be propitious, O Mother of the world. Be gracious, O Mother of the universe. Protect the universe. You are, O Devi, the ruler of all that is moving and unmoving.

You are the sole substratum of the world, because You subsist in the form of the earth. By You, who exist in the form of water, all this (universe) is gratified. O Devi of inviolable valor.

You are the power of Vishnu, and have endless valor. You are the primeval maya, which is the source of the universe; by You all this (universe) has been thrown into an illusion, O Devi. If You become gracious, You become the cause of final emancipation in this world.

All lores are Your aspects, O Devi; so are all women in the world, endowed with various attributes. By You alone, Mother, this world is filled. What praise can there be for You who are of the nature of primary and secondary expression regarding (objects) worthy of praise?

There was so much love and devotion in their melodious chanting of the Sanskrit slokas that some of them became very absorbed. Lost in their own world of ecstasy, they began displaying different gestures—stretching out their arms toward Amma, raising them high, joining the palms of their hands together and saluting Amma. Some shed tears of love as they continued singing the chant with tremendous devotion. The devotees were thrilled at the chance to sing for Amma. As Amma sat looking at them, compassion flowed from Her eyes. Her face shone like the full moon. Amma's mere glance with the bewitching smile She wore on Her lips threw a spell of enchantment over the devotees. Tears streamed down their cheeks as they soared to heights of supreme devotion while they continued to chant the hymn.

Amma sat very still on the cot. She manifested all the signs which She expresses during Devi Bhava—Her hands held in a divine mudra, a blissful smile radiating from Her face—as She gazed at the devotees who were chanting. A tidal wave of supreme devotion arose in them as their singing became more ecstatic and the entire hut vibrated to its fullness. Mother sat in that mood for some time, then She turned away from them but remained in an indrawn state. The chant slowly subsided. Perfect silence prevailed in the darshan hut. The devotees experienced the bliss of deep meditation. One of them was in a totally intoxicated mood. Filled with devotion and love, he cried and laughed at the same time as he called out 'Amma! Amma!' every now and then. Some of the devotees sat gazing at the Holy Mother's face. Nearly five minutes passed in this way before Amma slowly opened Her eyes chanting Shiva... Shiva... Shiva... Shiva... while moving Her right hand in circles, a familiar but incomprehensible gesture to the devotees.

Amma resumed receiving the devotees. The one who had asked the question about 'response' wanted to know more about it.

Amma responded in this manner: "You keep asking what response is and how to do it. Amma can speak to you about response. She might give you a convincing answer. But that won't help much. People are only interested in intellectually satisfying answers. Once they get such an answer, the mind will keep quiet for some time. And then again it will doubt; it will raise another objection or question. Thus, answers are often food for the mind. Every time you appease the hunger of the doubting mind, you only feed it with new ideas. This easily becomes a habit, and therefore, you never cultivate faith in your heart. You don't rely on your heart. And without faith and love, how can you ever learn to respond?

"Children, all great masters of the world, whether in the East or the West, teach us how to respond. They never react. Their whole life stands as a living witness for this great principle of life—response. Jesus Christ set an unforgettable example of how to respond. He let His body be tortured and crucified, and even when He was dying on the cross, Christ prayed for those who were against Him. He prayed for their own good—that they might be forgiven.

"When Kaikeyi, Sri Rama's step-mother, sought the boon of having Rama exiled to the forest for fourteen years, the Lord accepted the exile with a smile on His face. He was not at all hostile to Kaikeyi. Smilingly, He touched her feet, His heart overflowing with reverence and love. He simply accepted the exile as a fact; there was not a trace of anger within Him. Lakshmana, on the other hand, wanted to kill Kaikeyi for her cruel deed. When he heard about his elder brother's ill-fate, Lakshmana became fierce with anger and was determined to seek vengeance. He sought Rama's permission to imprison his own father, whom he called 'the unjust and henpecked king.' Lakshmana's reaction was terrible, whereas Rama responded beautifully. Rama's response, in fact, helped Lakshmana to calm down

"Even when engaged in active conflict, you can respond. In the battle between Rama and Ravana, the Lord killed Ravana's charioteer and his horses, destroyed the chariot and then disarmed Ravana completely. Having lost all hope for his life, Ravana stood waiting for Rama's sharp arrows to pierce his chest. But instead of the whir of arrows, he heard Rama's voice: "Ravana, I see you are completely disarmed." Rama's voice was calm, "I could finish you off now if I wanted to. But I won't. To kill someone who is disarmed and helpless goes against dharma. Therefore, go back to your palace, rest, treat your wounds, and come back tomorrow fresh and fully armed." What a great enemy Rama was! Even on the battlefield, even when Ravana had committed the unpardonable crime of kidnapping His divine consort and was standing in front of Him disarmed and totally helpless, Rama bore no malice but could speak such kind and wise words. This is response.

"Here is another example. When the hunter shot the sharp and deadly arrow which put an end to Krishna's body, the Lord did not react. He did not try to punish the hunter. On the contrary, Sri Krishna blessed the hunter with immortality. He bestowed on the hunter life's highest goal, mukti. This is response."

"It sounds like response is forgiveness," remarked the devotee who had asked the question.

"Forgiveness without having any feeling of anger or revenge is response," said Amma. "There are people who might forgive, but they still harbor intense hatred; they forgive but with vengeance in their hearts. For different reasons, people may sometimes appear to forgive. For example, one man beats another. The second man may not fight back because the first one is stronger. We cannot call this forgiveness. Though the second man does not retaliate, the fire of revenge may be raging in his mind. Likewise, when a father beats his son, or a teacher punishes a student, neither the son nor the student can return the blows. But they will feel a deep resentment within. This cannot be called forgiveness, for it is suppression of anger. It cannot be called response. Such unexpressed anger will remain deep within, and when the occasion arises, it will be expressed. That would be reaction, not response.

"There was a Mahatma who was a wandering monk. One day he was sitting under a tree when a hooligan happened to pass by and hit the monk with a cane. The stroke came down so hard on the monk's shoulder that the cane fell out of the hooligan's hand onto the ground. The Mahatma stood up and picked up the cane. Thinking that the monk was going to beat him back, the rascal ran away. The Mahatma ran after him. From at a distance some people had seen the hooligan beating the monk and came running. They stopped and seized the scoundrel. By that time the Mahatma had reached them with the cane in his hands. Handing the cane back to the hooligan, the Mahatma calmly said, 'I wanted to return your cane to you, that's all.' He turned to leave, but the people who had stopped the rogue said, 'What's going on? This blackguard just hit you hard on your shoulder. We saw it. He needs to be punished. You must hit him back—not once, but several times.' The Mahatma smiled and retorted, 'No, I can't. Why should I? He hit me and that's all right. I take it as a fact. But I do not understand why I should return the blow. What if one of the branches of that tree I was sitting under broke and fell on my body? I wouldn't pick up the branch and hit the tree back. Likewise, he hit me and I accept it. He did it out of ignorance. I should feel sympathy for his ignorance, not anger. I must have beaten him some time in a previous birth. And now I am experiencing the fruit of my action. In that sense it is not he who hit me, but it is my past which makes him hit me. Now if I hit him back, I would be creating more karma for myself. I would be adding more to the account I came here to close.' Having said this, the Mahatma walked away without another word.

"Children, response is an attitude. It happens when one is totally detached. This is possible only when one becomes free from the ego. Only egoless people can truly respond. Response happens when one reaches the state of no-mind. Mind and ego can only react. In fact, it is the mind and the ego that tempt one to react. They are the storehouse of the past. The past is the seat of negativity such as anger, hatred, revenge, attachment, and jealously. The past is the problem-creator. If the past doesn't exist for one, then no problems arise; only peace and bliss will exist. The past is the account into which we deposit more and more through our reactions. However, a Mahatma destroys the past completely and stops adding to his account. Once the past is gone, the ego is gone; the mind stuff is gone. Such a person cannot react. He can only respond, because all references cease to exist in him.

The past is the reference book. There is nothing to refer to once the past is removed."

This last remark raised a question, "The past is the reference book! What do you mean by that, Amma?"

Amma answered, "The past is a dictionary or a thesaurus. Whenever we hear, experience or do something, we automatically refer to these old pages. Through them we find meanings, interpretations or uses that were utilized before. Then we speak or act according to such references. This is reaction.

"For example, someone abuses us. Suddenly the past comes to the foreground. Even without waiting for our permission, even without our knowledge, it gives references. It says, 'You have been abused countless times by different people. Each time you were abused by someone, you retaliated. So do it again, abuse him back. Use stronger words and expressions.'

Thus, the chain of the past reveals itself: When someone offends you, you offend him in return. If someone gets angry at you, you return the anger. This is how it happens. The habitual reaction stored in the past comes up again and again. And each time you react, it becomes stronger and stronger. You and your victim each have a past. Both of you react to each other. The other person has also been abused a number of times. Each one reacts according to the strength and density of his past reactions. Both of you have volumes and volumes of giant-sized books to which you unknowingly refer. A Mahatma remains a blank sheet of paper, while an ordinary person keeps on writing on the pages, continuing to add to those gigantic books each time he reacts.

"Response comes from the great soul who remains blank. He does not want to disturb the silence with unnecessary sounds or disfigure the blank sheet of paper with unnecessary words. Response arises from a truly loving heart. Love cannot hurt; likewise, response cannot hurt."

All this time the young man who had feigned the neck pain sat quietly by Amma's side, listening as She spoke. All of a sudden, he prostrated at Mother's feet, weeping like a child. Amma lovingly drew him up and put his head on Her lap, once again displaying Her overflowing compassion and motherly love. The young man controlled his tears with great difficulty. Raising his head from Her lap, he said, "Amma, I want to be more courageous. I don't want to be a skeptic anymore. Sitting in your presence for only this long I have learned many things. I think I understand what I have been missing all my life. It is your love and compassion." He choked on his words, and once again his eyes filled with tears. He continued, "I don't want to miss you, Amma. I don't want to waste my life anymore." The young man covered his face and wept again.

As the darshan continued, the brahmacharis sang

Ini oru janmam

O Krishna, give me not another birth
Lest I fall into the deep quagmire of delusion.
If You give, then bestow the boon
To let me take birth as the servant
Of Your servants forever.

O Krishna, fill my mind with Your Holy Name
Reveal Your Lotus Feet bright and clear
Keep my mind ever equipoised
All should be felt as Your manifestation.

O Krishna, Treasure of Compassion
Salutations to You
With palms joined, I humbly salute You.

If I should get another birth,
Let it be beneficial to the world,
Giving the Imperishable Joy to others.
If You allow me that, then please give me
Any number of births as a human being.

Amma's response to this young man, Her expression of love and compassion toward him instead of condemning him for his deception, is clearly an example of how response can and does have a good influence on others. It produced such a positive change in his attitude, and this was witnessed by everybody present.

Amma's own life is a perfect example of how to respond rather than react. The early periods of Her life were filled with trials and tribulations. Except for a few people, everyone, including Her own family, turned against Her. A thousand young men joined together and formed an organization called 'The Committee To Stop Blind Faith.' Supported by some of the villagers and politicians, they tried to scandalize Amma. They tried to have Her imprisoned by accusing Her of crimes She hadn't committed; they used various mean and shabby methods trying to expose Her as a fraud. But Amma remained unperturbed. She never reacted to their torments and threats. She only prayed and cried to God, to Her Beloved Krishna, to the Divine Mother, seeking forgiveness for Her oppressors.

Even when She had to shoulder all the household chores and do all the work for others, Amma did not murmur any complaint. She always prayed, "O Lord, give me work; give me Your work." Amma worked ceaselessly. Even though She had so much to do, She would pray to God for more so that She could constantly dedicate every action to Him. Carrying water for cooking and pots of hot rice gruel on Her head, Amma even became bald in one spot. The hair fell out from the weight and heat of those pots. Nevertheless, She did not complain or stop working.

Amma's own parents and Her older brother were antagonistic toward Her. Her brother always taunted Her, usually for no reason. Amma's mother, Damayanti, was a strict disciplinarian and not at all lenient with Her. Amma lived in the midst of all these adverse circumstances, responding beautifully to all the situations that arose in Her life, constantly focusing Her mind on the Supreme Being.

It would be beneficial to recall another incident when Amma responded to a man who constantly used to abuse Her. He was a notorious rowdy of the village where Amma was born. Ever since Amma manifested Her Divinity to the world, he had an antagonistic attitude toward Her. Whenever he got a chance, he abused and scandalized Her, but Amma never had any ill feelings towards him. It was Her nature to take everything as the benevolence of Divine Providence.

One day as Amma was on Her way to a devotee's house, She found the rowdy standing at the boat jetty. A contagious type of scabies covered his body. Pus and blood were oozing out of the sores. His body was dirty and smelly. Amma went up to him and lovingly inquired about his disease. Holding both his hands, She compassionately soothed the scabies. Obtaining some sacred ash from Gayatri, Amma rubbed it on his sores. The sympathy and concern She expressed towards this man was so great that one would think that he were a close devotee. Before She left him, Amma held both his hands affectionately and kissed the back of his hands. Now the notorious man could not help crying; he sobbed like a child. Once again Amma expressed Her love for him, wiping his tears, and then went on Her way. After this incident, the man became an ardent devotee of Amma. This is a perfect demonstration of how response, rather than reaction, can create a miraculous change response creates, even in the worst type of people.

Mother says, "We should try to see the nature of things as they are. The nature of anything, whether an object or a being, cannot be other than the way it is. If this is understood, one can only respond. One can only pray for the good of others, and feel sympathy and love. Frogs croak and crickets chirp at night. That is their nature; they cannot do otherwise. They are not going to change even if you get angry at them. Nobody stays awake at night saying, 'I'm not getting proper sleep because of this noise.' People simply ignore them and go to bed because they know that frogs croak and crickets chirp. They know that it is the nature of those creatures and they cannot be otherwise.

"Likewise, each person has his own nature. Through your anger, you cannot change the nature of other people. Only love can change them. Understand this, and try to feel love and sympathy for all. Be compassionate, even toward those who bother you. Pray for them. Such an attitude will also help your mind to remain calm and peaceful. This is genuine response."

It was twelve o'clock. There were still many people waiting to have Amma's darshan. Amma continued receiving Her children as the brahmacharis sang

Mano buddhya

I am neither the mind, intellect, ego nor memory,
Neither ears nor tongue
Nor the senses of smell and sight;
Nor am I ether, earth, fire, water or air.
I am Pure Awareness-Bliss, I am Shiva! I am Shiva!

I am neither the life force nor the five vital airs;
Neither the body's seven elements nor its sheaths;
Nor hands nor feet nor tongue,

Nor the organs of sex and voiding;
I am Pure Awareness-Bliss, I am Shiva! I am Shiva!

Neither loathing nor liking have I,
Neither greed nor delusion;
No sense have I of ego or pride,
Neither religious merit nor wealth,
Neither enjoyment nor Liberation have I;
I am Pure Awareness-Bliss, I am Shiva! I am Shiva!

Neither right nor wrongdoing am I
Neither pleasure nor pain; nor the mantra,
Nor the sacred place, the Vedas, the sacrifice;
Neither the act of eating, the eater, nor the food;
I am Pure Awareness-Bliss, I am Shiva! I am Shiva!

Chapter 7

Soon after the morning meditation some of the brahmacharis were discussing Amma's satsang on 'response and reaction.' Since most of them were educated young men, each one was making comments, giving different interpretations of Amma's words, each according to his own understanding and intellectual capacity. A brahmachari said, "I don't think that a person who lives in society or a person who has a responsible job can always respond. He has to react. For example, how can a business executive or an administrator in the government avoid reacting? If the business executive only responds and never reacts, the company will not function properly and it will have to close down. If a government administrator only responds and never reacts, the government will be a mess. Being in a position of responsibility, he has to discipline others; and to discipline others requires a certain amount of reaction. To make others obey, reaction is necessary; otherwise, one cannot function properly in society. Yesterday Amma gave the examples of Rama, Krishna and Christ, but even they had to react on certain occasions, didn't they?"

Another brahmachari gave his opinion: "I think that the instructions Amma gave yesterday are meant for serious sadhaks. What She said was intended for those who are inclined to lead a spiritual life, renouncing all worldly desires. The ego is necessary for living in the world. When there is an ego, one cannot respond; one can only react. Amma Herself stressed that point."

Still another brahmachari wanted to have his turn. He began, "I think..."

He was interrupted by a voice , "Don't think!"

Startled, they all looked up. Amma was standing on the balcony. "Don't think!" She shouted down to them. "Children, you just finished meditation and already you've started thinking—just the opposite of meditation. You practice meditation to sublimate all thoughts, to cease your thinking. But here you are, brain-storming about something that should be practiced, not discussed."

Amma continued, "Children, you all think. You all have different views and opinions, but response comes only when you stop thinking, only when all your views and opinions disappear. Here each one of you is 'thinking' deeply. Whatever little energy you may have gained through meditation has been dissipated due to this senseless thinking. It is just like wasting hard-earned money on peanuts. What a pity! Go and do something useful."

The brahmacharis dispersed quickly. Amma retraced Her steps to Her room.

The ability to respond while living in the world

Two hours after the above incident took place, Amma was sitting on the bottom step of the staircase leading to Her room. Just behind Amma sat Gayatri and Kunjumol. After being chided earlier in the morning, the brahmacharis who had taken part in the discussion felt a little guilty and were restless. They all stood at a distance from where Amma was sitting, not daring to come any closer. Seeing their hesitation, Amma called them to come. Having offered their prostrations, they all sat on the ground in front of Amma. For some time Amma did not say anything, but

Her face had an expression of extraordinary depth. The brahm-acharis looked a bit perplexed, not knowing what She was going to say or do. After a short while, Amma spoke: "What was the discussion about this morning?"

Amma's voice was very calm, Her countenance full of love and peace. The brahmacharis relaxed a little, yet out of fear they did not answer Amma's question. She encouraged them saying, "Do not feel frightened. Amma is not angry with you. How can She be angry? Why do you think that Amma would get angry with you? Speak up. What were you discussing?"

Amma's soothing words gave them the courage to speak, and one of them explained to Her the things they had discussed. A big smile lit up Her face as She lovingly glanced at Her children and said, "It is true that a person cannot completely put away his ego when he is living in society. He does have to react. He may have to talk in a rough language, or he may have to take a tough stand at times. But, so what! How can that create a hindrance to responding? What do you mean by saying that response is not at all possible just because someone is a business executive or a government administrator? Response is possible if one tries. It is a positive mental attitude you develop toward others, whether friend or enemy.

"Response is to stand aside and be untouched, unaffected and detached. But usually, if you get into a disagreement or quarrel with someone, or when you try to discipline someone, you react because you are involved and identified with it. When you get angry, you become identified with your anger and cannot be detached. You cannot see the anger arising in you. Instead, you become the anger. Externally, great souls may sometimes act like ordinary human beings, but internally they always remain apart from the actions they perform. Detachment is the very core of their lives. They cannot react because they are detached. Reactions occur because people are attached to their actions. Attachment to the work and its fruit creates ego, which will destroy the ability to respond. Detachment from the work and its fruit destroys the ego, which will help one to respond. Attachment fills the mind with more thoughts and desires, which will only cause reactions. Detachment empties the mind of all thoughts and desires, which allows response to take place.

"Children, try to perform your work with detachment. In this way, you will learn to respond. You can scold someone and still be detached. You can discipline someone and yet remain detached. That is why Amma said response is a mental attitude, that it is purely subjective. One who watched Rama or Krishna might have thought that they were reacting to their respective opponents. Indeed, Rama killed Ravana for abducting His wife, Sita. He killed many other demons as well. One might also think Krishna reacted when He killed Kamsa or when He sided with the Pandavas to help destroy the Kauravas. But to make this kind of judgment is wrong. Rama was ready to accept Ravana the person, but not his ego. Krishna was ready to accept the Kauravas, but not their egos. Ravana's ego was dangerous to society. The egos of Duryodhana and of those who sided with him were also dangerous to society; therefore, Krishna had to destroy them. As a king it was Rama's duty to destroy the egos that could harm to the entire world. It was not only because Ravana had kidnapped Sita that Rama had to kill him, but because the latter had become a threat to the whole world. By killing him, Rama was saving the world from demonic hands. Rama was only protecting and preserving dharma.

"The apparent ego that each one of them wore was only a mask—a mask with which they never identified, and which they could remove at any time. They always knew that they were different from the mask, that the mask was not who they really were.

"One should be careful not to mistake the masks for their real nature. One needs a very subtle eye to penetrate and see their real nature. Even Arjuna, Krishna's closest disciple and friend, took Krishna's mask to be real. Only once, when the Lord Himself blessed him with divine sight, did Arjuna see who Krishna really was. Even Lakshmana, the dearest brother of Rama, did not see Him accurately. To be able to discern divinity requires an exceptionally subtle eye. It requires a subtle way of looking to see divine beings. But to see them, in fact, is not seeing—it is experiencing. To experience them one must enter into them, into their real Being. If you have the subtle eye to see them, or if you have the experience of entering into their real Being, then you know that they never react.

"Remember, the same Rama who killed Ravana, and who killed thousands of fully-armed demons in a few seconds, could also remain unmoved and unperturbed like a mountain when Kaikeyi took away the kingdom that was rightfully His, and sent Him into exile. Rama was not impatient. Neither was he a coward. He was as fierce as the fire of dissolution. Recall His fierce form when the ocean would not yield to Him. He was about to dry up the entire ocean. Such was His strength. So if He wanted to, He could have easily regained His kingdom. But He did not do that. Instead, He responded. He accepted. See the beauty of it.

"For some people, apparent response is born not out of love and detachment, but out of cowardice and timidity. There is no beauty in this sort of apparent response. This is how a weakling behaves. He is passive; he is motivated by fear. But when God, the Governor of the entire universe and the most powerful Being responds, there is immense beauty in it, for it is an edifying experience."

A five-year old boy, who was the son of a devotee, happened to be among those who had gathered around Amma. One of the brahmacharis told Amma that the boy had sung bhajans beautifully the previous day. Amma looked at him and smilingly asked, "Is this true, son?" The boy nodded his head. In a begging tone, Amma asked him to sing a kirtan. Without the least shyness, the boy sang *Vedambike*

> *O Mother of the Vedas*
> *O Mother of Sounds, I bow to You.*
> *I bow to Your Feet, adored by the Gods.*

> *Bestowing love*
> *Bestowing the radiance of the lotus*
> *O Lover of music*
> *Take me across this ocean of misery.*

> *O Goddess of Wisdom*
> *O Parvati Who does good to all the world*
> *Destroyer of pride and rebirth*
> *Be victorious.*

> *Mother is the Life of all creatures*
> *Mother is the Cause of all things.*
> *Bowing to You with palms joined*
> *I pray, give me Liberation*
> *O Powerful One*
> *Great Radiance, I bow to You.*

For some time Amma gazed intently at the boy as he was singing. Then She became indrawn and this state lasted until the end of the song. When the boy finished singing, Amma called him to come to Her. She embraced him tightly as She kissed him on both cheeks, telling him, "How beautifully you sang, Amma's darling son!" Amma seated him next to Her. She asked Kunjumol to bring some toffees. When Kunjumol brought a bag of toffees, Amma took a few and gave them to the boy.

Having not yet received an answer on how a person can respond while doing his duties in the world, the resident who asked the question about response now raised the point again.

Amma answered, "Children, even if you live in the world as an executive or an administrator, you can still learn to respond, provided you develop and cultivate detachment. The business executive or the governmental administrator should discharge his duties sincerely. If the need arises he should be able to take a tough stand. If the workers become lazy or if they try to cheat the company, of course the executive must have the courage and confidence to rise to the situation and take necessary action against them.

"You can be angry with the laziness of a worker but not with the worker himself. The humanity in the worker, the consciousness in the worker, should be respected because it is not different from yours. In that sense you and he are equals. Don't get angry with the person. Getting angry will shatter your clarity of vision.

"Amma does not understand why you should react and allow your mind to sink into a mire of hellish thoughts. Reaction builds up hatred. Hatred makes the mind a hell. Likewise, anger, jealousy and uncontrollable craving for name and fame make life equal to hell. You lose your peace of mind. You lose the love and beauty within you, and your mind becomes a madhouse. Whether you are a business executive or the supreme sovereign of a country, to react will only create chaos and confusion within you. The very thought of reacting will cloud your vision. You will lose your discrimination. You will not be able to do your work properly. You may do the wrong thing which could destroy the reputation of the company.

"To make an intelligent decision one needs to be even-minded. What you call presence of mind is a state of mind in which one doesn't become agitated but remains well-balanced, even in the midst of severe problems. A person who reacts thoughtlessly cannot be a good ruler or a good professional in any field of work. He will be a failure in any position of responsibility. His uncontrolled reactions will pull him away from all good fortune or favorable opportunities, and from all good things that can happen in life.

"Let's come down closer to our lives. When we come down to the level of ordinary human beings, we can see that knowingly or unknowingly we do respond in our everyday life. But this is not a totally reactionless state. It is controlled reaction—something important is at stake and so you react without being carried away by anger. Internally you may still have negative feelings, but externally you control them to a certain extent, for otherwise, it could create a disaster. A government official can do this for the sake of his country, and an executive can do it for the sake of the company.

"Suppose you are the head of a large firm, and there are demands being made by the workers. The leader of the protesting workers is threatening to call a strike. You personally feel that his demands are unreasonable and that his tactics are unfair, even offensive. In this kind of situation the predominant emotion that bubbles up in your mind will be anger. But you don't show it, because, if you did, it could worsen the situation. Therefore, you try to control your anger and resentment. You try not to return those negative feelings 'in the same coin,' for if you do, it could result in a disaster. You remember when you had a similar experience in the past. You suddenly become aware of the same pattern from the past.

"Previously you could not control your anger toward the agitators. You were rash in your behavior and used extreme measures. The opposition reacted with even greater force. That previous incident affected the entire company. You lost your peace of mind, and your personal family life was disrupted. You now remember what happened that time and how the chain of events resulted in disaster.

"This memory brings you back to your senses. You do not want to do that again. You do not want to create unnecessary trouble and thereby lose your peace of mind. The last time due to your uncontrollable outburst the company closed down for several months. Many families suffered and you lived in fear and dread of what others might do to you in retaliation. In remembering the adverse consequences which were caused by your uncontrollable reactions, you become discriminative. You control your anger and volatile nature; you calm down and put a big smile on your face. You meet with the leader of the protesters and treat him cordially, inviting him to your office where you offer him a cup of coffee. You express your concern for the welfare of the employees. With deliberate caution you explain the company's situation and assure him that you will do everything in your power to come to an appropriate agreement with the protesters. This way of tackling the problems in your life, whether in your professional life or in your personal family life, can be called a response. In this case, you are reacting too, but it does not hurt the other person, because the anger within you is not expressed. You give him the feeling that you are concerned about him and his problems. You create a positive feeling in the other man's heart.

"However, if you investigate closely, you will see that deep down this is still a reaction because the anger is still within you. You have suppressed it to prevent yourself from expressing it. But you haven't done anything to exhaust it. Many circumstances like this arise in one's life, and each time you do the same thing. The chain of these events becomes longer and longer. Externally, you may look as if you are responding, but internally you are not. It is only the suppression of your reactions followed by giving an external impression of responding.

"Children, it does not matter who or what you are, if you really want to you can master the art of response. An executive or an administrator responds during certain situations in which he is required to act diplomatically without expressing any negative feelings. He could therefore do it also in any other situation, provided he has the determination and sincere interest to practice response. He has the potential to do it. He just has to work on it. He just has to do some practice to digest and assimilate the residue collected within, which has been left behind by such incidents. Once you learn to remove the residue of suppressed anger and desire for revenge, you are transformed into a fountain of tremendous energy with which you can accomplish even so-called impossible tasks. The executive or administrator has the power or mental capacity to do it. Whether he will practice it or not is another question. However, a certain amount of detachment and love is necessary to have the attitude of response."

Yet another question was asked: "What is the difference between this seeming response of an executive and the sadhak who learns to respond genuinely?"

"Children, a spiritual seeker, who strives hard to attain the state of perfection will also have anger and hatred within him. There will be situations in which he loses control of his mind as well. Like the executive (in the example above) who has learned from his past mistakes of uncontrollable reactions, the sadhak also makes use of the remembrance of past experiences to discriminate and control himself. But unlike the executive, the sadhak constantly works on his anger and strives hard to get rid of such tendencies. Through incessant practice, keeping his mind fixed on the goal of Self-realization, he sublimates his negative emotions, and in due course, the anger and other negative feelings are uprooted.

"The difference is that while the spiritual seeker feels that eliminating anger is essential to his life, someone like an administrator or an executive, for example, feels it is part of his professional life to keep his anger under control. His aim is to tackle that particular situation, and that is the end of it. He may be able to control his anger when a provocative situation arises, but the anger that has arisen within him filters deep into his mind and gets deposited there, waiting for the opportunity to express itself again.

"Like the executive, the sadhak also may not express anger at the moment he is provoked. Or, under certain circumstances when it becomes uncontrollable, he may express it; but later he will meditate, pray and chant his mantra to remove the anger and its very cause. As far as a sadhak is concerned, removing anger and other negative tendencies is his life's goal. His entire life is dedicated toward that. Therefore, he works hard to eliminate the ego and all its different aspects. Eventually his constant effort and the Guru's grace take him to the state of perfection—where there is no ego, no thoughts and no mind. Once he reaches that state he will be able to genuinely respond."

As the explanation progressed, another question came up, "Amma, from your explanations I get the impression that response is a state where there is neither action nor reaction. Is that correct?"

Amma answered, "Yes, in the ultimate sense there is no action or reaction. There is only the witness-consciousness attitude. You may appear to act or react, but there is neither action or reaction. You simply watch in silence while your body acts or reacts.

" A genuine response takes place only when you become completely free from the grip of the ego, when you become nothing or nobody. Until then, the ego is hidden behind all your actions, reactions, and seeming responses.

"This is the highest state one can attain. There is no point beyond that. This state is the 'pointless point.' To attain this state one must do intense spiritual practices."

Amma wanted to hear a newly composed song. The brahmacharis sang it

Katinnu katayai

O Mother who shines as the Ear of the ear,
Mind of the mind and Eye of the eye,
You are the Life of life
And Your Being is Life of the Living.

As the ocean is to the waves,
You are the Soul of souls
You are the Nectar of the nectar or knowledge,
O Mother! Pearl of the Immortal Self are You
And the Essence of Bliss,
Great Maya You are and the Absolute Itself.

Neither can eyes reach You
Nor can the mind grasp You
Words are hushed in Your Presence, O Mother.
Who says they have seen You have really not,
As You, O Great Goddess, are beyond intellect.

Sun, moon and stars shine not of themselves
But are illumined by Your Brilliance,
Through discrimination the courageous can tread
The path to the Abode of Eternal Peace,
The Supreme Truth.

It was a sunny day. Mother was sitting on the staircase facing the backwaters which marked the Ashram's southern boundary. A few children from the fishing village were trying to catch fish in these waters. Two of them were standing on the shore holding a clay pot, while another, who seemed a little older, moved silently in the water trying to catch the fish with his bare hands. Now and then he dived deep into the murky backwaters, surfacing after a short while with one or two fish in his hands. Amma was looking intently at the children. She said, "Look at those children. They are the ones who look after their family. Everyday they catch fish like this with their bare hands. They sell the fish to other people or in the market, and with that hard-earned money these small children buy the necessary foodstuffs for their family. Au such a young age they are burdened with supporting the family."

There was deep concern in Her voice. Amma called to the two who were holding the pot. They approached and stood in front of Amma. "Did you have a good catch today?" She asked them. "No," replied the children. The older of the two said, "Because of the rain, the water has risen very high, making it hard for our brother to catch enough fish."

Amma looked into the pot. It contained only a few small fish. She looked towards the water and at the other boy. The oldest brother was still diving in the water, feeling about with his hands in search of fish. He had no success. Amma turned around and whispered something to Kunjumol, who got up and left.

A few minutes later, Kunjumol returned with a plastic bag containing a few apples, a bunch of bananas, some sweets and other foodstuffs. In addition to these items Amma gave them a package of rice and fresh vegetables, enough for a family to cook one or two dishes. The children were overwhelmed with joy. They smiled heartily and called out to their brother, "Anna, Anna," (elder brother), Ammachi has given us enough food. Let's stop fishing and go home." "Really?" he asked, coming out of the water. After seeking Amma's permission, the three of them happily returned home.

Love and compassion

Wednesday, 25 July, 1984

It was almost midday. Mother was sitting in Br. Nealu's hut peeling tapioca root. This was the first hut built in the Ashram where Amma, along with Gayatri, had lived for nearly two years. In those days, part of the hut was also used as a storeroom and kitchen to cook food for Amma and the first group of brahmacharis.

Late in the morning, Amma returned from a neighboring devotee's house with some tapioca root in Her hands. Holding it up in front of everyone, She said like an innocent child, "This Amma plucked Herself from their plot. Now She is going to cook it. Once it is cooked, Amma will give it to all Her children."

Amma insisted on peeling and cooking it Herself. While She was peeling and preparing the tapioca root, one of the brahmacharis asked, "Amma, is love and compassion the same thing, or are they different?"

"When love becomes Divine Love, compassion also fills the heart. Love is the inner feeling, and compassion its expression. Compassion is expressing your heartfelt concern for someone—for a suffering human being. Therefore, love and compassion are two sides of the same coin—they co-exist.

"There is love and Love. You love your family, but you do not love your neighbor. You love your son or daughter, but you do not love all children. You love your father and mother, but you do not love everyone the way you love your father and mother. You love your religion, but you do not love all religions.

Likewise, you have love for your country, but you do not love all countries. Hence, this is not true Love; it is only limited love. The transformation of this limited love into Divine Love is the goal of spirituality. In the fullness of Love blossoms the beautiful, fragrant flower of compassion.

"Love with a small 'I' is limited. It exists in its own small world. It cannot contain more than a few people and a few things. It is narrow and is always changing. It has no peaks. The apparent peaks are not the highest pinnacles. They are only raised a little above ground level, just a little. Soon those little peaks will turn to plain, flat ground. There are ups and downs in love. In due course, all the 'ups' will disappear and there will only be 'downs.' This changeable love can become permanent love only when the feeling of 'I' and 'mine' disappears.

"As long as there is the feeling of 'I,' there is also the feeling of 'you;' thus love always has a personal touch. It occurs between two people. In order to love there must be two. Love becomes impersonal only when the two disappear. In that state of Oneness there is a constant flow of Love. From then on Love starts flowing from its very source. As it flows, it does not think of the other end. The flow of Love is unobstructed, just like the flow of the river. The river cannot but flow. The river does not think of the other end, the ocean. The merging just happens in the course of its flow. In that merging there are no calculations at all. Likewise, the sun just shines. It does not think about touching the earth with its rays; the contact just happens.

"In the same way, when the obstructions of the ego, fear, and the feeling of otherness disappear, you cannot do anything but Love; and you do not expect anything in return. You don't care about receiving—you just flow. Whoever comes into the river of Love will be bathed in it, whether the person is healthy or diseased, a man or a woman, wealthy or poor. Anyone can take any number of dips in it. Whether somebody bathes in it or not, the river of Love does not care. If somebody criticizes or abuses the river of Love, it does not care; it simply flows. When that constant flow of Love overflows and is expressed through every word and deed we call it compassion.

"Compassion is Pure Consciousness expressed through your words and actions. Compassion is the art of non-hurting, for compassion cannot hurt. Compassion cannot hurt anyone because compassion is the manifestation of consciousness, and consciousness cannot hurt anyone. Just as open space of the infinite sky cannot hurt anyone, compassion, the manifestation of consciousness cannot hurt anyone. One who has compassion can only be compassionate.

"Compassion does not see the faults of others. It does not see the weaknesses of people. It makes no distinction between good and bad people. Compassion cannot draw a line between two countries, two faiths or two religions. Compassion has no ego; thus there is no fear, lust or passion. Compassion simply forgives and forgets. Compassion is like a passage. Everything passes through it. Nothing can stay there. Compassion is love expressed in all its fullness."

A question was interjected, "That is what a real spiritual master has, doesn't he?

"Yes," replied Amma, "a real spiritual master is both Love and compassion in all fullness. Sometimes his love manifests as discipline. Normally a certain amount of pain is experienced when one is being disciplined, but the Guru's compassion removes it. When you correct someone or when you scold someone, his ego is hurt; his individuality is crushed. That is what people dislike the most. They do not want to be called to question or be corrected even if they are wrong. So there is pain in being disciplined. Whether it is the father disciplining the son, the mother disciplining the daughter, or the teacher disciplining the student, pain is unavoidable. The latter will feel hurt by the former, and in many cases he will react. In some cases even though one feels hurt, he will not express his reaction. He may obey but, at the same time, feel tremendously angry within. There will be great pain inside. He may want to protest, but due to fear he will not do anything. This may continue, and pain, hurt feelings, anger and hatred will accumulate in his mind. At some point this accumulation of negative emotions will explode. It is unfortunate that this happens in the ordinary process of trying to discipline another, even when it comes out of love. Even if the disciplining is born of the father's or mother's love, this pain will sometimes remain unhealed.

"On the other hand, in a Guru-sishya relationship, there are no hurt feelings in the disciple's mind. There is no pain, no deep wounds, no anger or hatred in the disciple's mind. The reason is that the sishya accepts the Guru's disciplining and scolding with a positive attitude. He surrenders to the Guru fully. He knows that whatever the Guru does is for his highest good. But the most important factor is the Guru's compassion which has tremendous healing power. All the pain, anger, hatred and other negativity will be healed by the Guru's compassion. Sometimes the sishya may feel hurt; he may feel angry toward the Guru when the Guru scolds or disciplines him. But the Guru's overflowing compassion heals these wounds, helping the disciple to become positive. The Guru's compassion overlooks the disciple's anger and hatred; the Guru's compassion forgives all. That supreme compassion encompasses the disciple completely and soothes all the negative feelings.

"This soothing effect of the Guru's compassion helps the sishya feel relaxed and at ease. In this way he is able to receive and absorb the Guru's disciplining with a positive attitude. The compassion makes the disciple feel that he is a part of the Guru, that he is the Guru's own, that the Guru loves him immensely and that the Guru does everything for his highest good. Feeling the flow of compassion from the Guru and observing his renunciation and selflessness, the disciple knows that the Guru cannot be selfish at all. Thus the sishya will not accumulate any negative feelings, even though he may feel pain or anger from time to time. Thus the Guru can discipline the disciple without letting any trace of the disciple's reactions remain within. The father or mother cannot remove the traces of reaction from the mind of their son or daughter because they have no compassion. Because Love has not fully bloomed in them, they are egoistic in their words and actions, and thus they force discipline onto their children; they force their own ideas onto them, most of the time ignoring the children's feelings. However, the Guru cannot force discipline onto his disciples because he is not a person. He is not the body; he is not the ego. He is consciousness.

"After chastising or punishing the son or daughter for his or her mistakes, the father or mother may call and treat their child in a very loving way. But the thought that they have scolded him and forced him to obey remains in the child's mind. Parents really do this; they force their children to do things in a certain way, rather than setting an example for them. They cannot be otherwise because they are limited individuals. They are operating from their egos. When they operate from their egos, they cannot but try to force their own will on another, even though they do it in the name of love. In the name of love, they force their egos on their child. The child feels it, so afterwards, even if they treat him lovingly or affectionately, the hurt feelings in the child remain unchanged. The anger and hatred remain; they are not eliminated.

"In the Guru-sishya relationship, however, this is different. After disciplining the disciple through his pure love, the Guru makes him feel at ease and comfortable by expressing his compassion toward him in great measure. This helps the disciple to be a very good receiver, a very good container; thus, he can continue to be receptive and positive.

"In the Guru-sishya relationship there is no forcing. The disciple's inner thirst to go beyond the limitations of his ego, and the Guru's selfless Love and compassionate guidance help the sishya refrain from building up anger within him.

"When one lives in Love, when one's whole being transforms itself into Love, he becomes compassionate. Love fills the heart and overflows as compassion. In that state when the mind and mental thoughts are completely consumed by the fire of Supreme Love, when the seeker's mind becomes like space, the thing that brings him down is compassion. The quality that makes the soul feel the call of those who are groping in darkness is compassion. That which keeps the body of the Mahatma in this world of plurality is compassion. Love and compassion are basically the same; they are two sides of the same coin."

Mother stopped for a while and during this time a brahmachari spontaneously sang a song in praise of Amma, *Kannadachalum turannalum*. As he sang, the brahmachari shed tears of joy and devotion

Kannadachalum turannalum

My Mother ever resides
In my eyes, open or closed.

With glances pouring forth compassion,
She hugs one and all.

Melting the heart with a shower of love,
My Mother is indeed an Ocean of Joy.

A robber or a tyrant, in front of Mother,
Both are Her darling children.
Whether She is despised or adored,
Love streams forth from Mother.

Enjoyed by the tongue, sweetness is not perfect,
Perfect sweetness is the love of God
And the sense to enjoy that
Comes only through my Mother.

At the end of the song, the brahmachari, with a choking throat said, "Oh, Amma, may your compassion and grace guide us forever on the path of spirituality. Without your grace we cannot reach the other shore."

Amma was very pleased with his innocence, but She jokingly retorted, "Your Mother is not compassionate. She is a demon. Be careful. She is a tough guy." Everybody laughed at Amma's playful threat.

The satsang continued, "Certainly, the greatness of our ancient saints and sages is indescribable. Without their compassion today's world would be hell. It is their renunciation and compassion which sustain today's world. All the unrighteous actions performed by selfish and wicked people are balanced by the compassionate and loving actions performed by the spiritual beings who are the world's only real benefactors. Their compassion surpasses our understanding; it flows even to those who try to destroy them.

"Amma will tell you a story. Once a king brought the prince, his only son, to the hermitage of a great saint. There the young prince was to be imbued with the knowledge of the Vedas and other scriptural texts. That was the kind of education that existed in those days. Whether a prince or a layman, a young person underwent several years of education and discipline under the guidance of a master. During this period students had to stay with the master without having any contact with their own parents or family.

"When the king and son arrived at the hermitage, all was quiet; no one seemed to be there. Looking around, they finally found the saint seated under a tree. He was deep in samadhi—totally absorbed and oblivious to his surroundings. When the saint finally emerged from his meditation, he immediately bowed to the king and offered him a seat.

"The king, however, did not feel that he had been received in the proper manner, especially since he had to go around looking for the saint and then had to wait for him to come out of meditation. His self-image as king was wounded, for he was used to being waited on. He could not tolerate having to wait for others. He felt it was humiliating to have to wait for other people; after all, he was king and they should always be ready to serve him. His ego was hurt and he began to boil with anger. He glared at the saint, trying to contain the rage building within him.

" 'Your royal highness,' the saint spoke very politely, 'may I know the purpose of your visit?'

At this point, the king's anger erupted, 'What?! Are you trying to mock me? Even without receiving me properly, you are asking the purpose of my visit? Where are all the residents of this ashram? Where are your disciples?' He added sarcastically, 'Can't I have their darshan too?'

"The saint apologized for not providing the king with a proper reception. He explained that since this was a school for discipline, the students are taught to adhere strictly to their scheduled routine of study, work, performing religious rites and sadhana. 'I myself was in meditation,' the saint said.

"At this remark the king raged with fury. He shouted, 'Are you also trying to insult me?'

"Seeing that his words only provoked the angry king, the saint did not speak anymore. He just sat calmly and quietly.

"Furious as he was, the king managed to suppress his anger when he recalled the purpose of his visit. He remembered that he had come to have his son educated by this saint. Though he was angry because his ego was wounded, the king brought his temper under control. He did not want to spoil the chance for the prince to have a first-rate education under the guidance of this master who had the highest reputation in the land for his wisdom and knowledge. Therefore, he suddenly put on a show of humility, apologized for his emotional outburst and requested the great master to accept his son as a disciple.

"The saint, who was the embodiment of patience and forgiveness, readily agreed and accepted the prince as a sishya. When the arrangements were completed, the king took leave of the saint with a smiling face but a wounded ego.

"The prince was a brilliant student and a good disciple. His obedience, discipline and devotion to the Guru made him the saint's favorite. Twelve long years rolled by as the saint taught him everything he knew. The prince not only became a real master in all the scriptures but also in using all weapons. Although he had now become a handsome youth, the prince was very humble and remained an obedient and devoted disciple of the great saint.

"At last the prince's education was completed, and the day to take leave of his beloved and revered Guru arrived. With a heavy heart and eyes filled with tears, the prince stood in front of the great master. With humility and gratitude he addressed his Guru, 'O Holy One, my beloved master, I am yours. Whatever I have belongs to you. I am nothing before your glory. How can I ever repay you for all your love and compassion? This humble servant is waiting to hear from you. What should I offer as Gurudakshina?'

"The great saint affectionately caressed his beloved disciple. Tears of joy rolled down his cheeks as he said, 'My child, my son, your obedience, humility and the great love that you have had for me are your Gurudakshina. You have already made your offering my son, you have already given it.'

"But the prince lovingly insisted that the saint should accept something from him as dakshina: 'Let it be anything, O Venerable One, even if it is my own life. I am ready to lay it at your holy feet.' Embracing his dear student, the saint told him that he did not want anything right at that moment but would definitely ask when the appropriate time came. With the permission and blessing of the saint, the prince returned to the kingdom to live with his parents, the king and the queen.

"The spiteful king had been waiting for the day when his son would return after having finished his studies. The prince had not been back for a day when the king, whose mind was bent on revenge for the humiliation his ego had suffered, sent his soldiers to burn down the saint's hermitage. The saint and the hermits were severely tortured by the soldiers and abandoned in the forest without any food, clothing or shelter. Hearing his soldiers' report on how well they had carried out his commands, the cruel, egoistic king felt happy, thinking that he had taught a good lesson to the saint by 'getting even with him.'

"A few days after this incident, the king announced he would soon retire and his son would be crowned king. Before his coronation, the prince wanted to have the permission and blessing of his beloved master before entering this new phase of his life. Mounting a steed, he rode to the hermitage, totally unaware of his father's cruel deed. Alighting from the horse, the prince wondered whether he had lost his way and reached another place. The spot where the hermitage had been looked deserted.

"After wandering around for a while, he found his beloved master sitting under a banyan tree deeply absorbed in meditation. Now as he looked around, he could easily see that the hermitage had recently been burned down. The prince waited until the master arose from meditation. When the saint finally opened his eyes, the prince prostrated before him and inquired what had happened to the hermitage. 'Nothing, my son,' replied the great soul, 'some forest fire. Don't bother about it. Tell me what brought you here.'

"The prince sensed that something was wrong. Repeatedly he pleaded with the master to disclose to him what had really happened, but the saint would not speak. Finally the other students of the hermitage relented and revealed the truth to him. Upon hearing the horrible story, the prince went into a state of shock and was even momentarily paralyzed. Coming back to consciousness, the prince gnashed his teeth in anger. His right hand automatically moved to the handle of his sheathed sword, and the next moment the infuriated prince leaped on his horse. 'Coward, you are dead,' he roared and began to charge off.

"With lightning movement, the saint jumped in front of the horse. He tried to stop the prince, but the prince was fierce. All the saint's attempts to calm him down failed. All his advice and warnings fell on deaf ears. The prince was beside himself with anger and determined to avenge the wrong done to his master by his father. Finally the saint said, 'All right, you can go. But before you leave I wish to have the Gurudakshina that you promised. I want it right now!'

"Hearing these words of his Guru, the prince alighted from the horse and prayed to the Guru to ask whatever he desired. The great saint smilingly replied, 'I want you to free your father from this punishment that you are about to give him. That is the Gurudakshina I want from you.' This rendered the prince speechless and all he could do was to gaze at the radiant and compassionate face of his Guru. The next moment he burst into tears and fell prostrate at the great saint's holy feet."

Thus, Amma finished the story. The way She had presented it was so alive and powerful that it created an atmosphere saturated with divine love and compassion. Deeply touched, the brahmacharis and the two brahmacharinis, silently shed tears, for they truly felt and experienced the compassion of the saint in the story. A long meditative silence followed. This was so powerful and overpowering that nobody could speak or move for some time. It was as if the experience of compassion had made everything stand still.

A few more minutes passed. Then Gayatri's voice broke the silence, "The tapioca root is cooked and ready to be served." Amma distributed a few pieces to each one of Her children. As She was serving them, Amma said, "It is very hot. Careful, don't burn your mouth." Thus, after bestowing upon Her children another fond memory to cherish, Amma left the hut.

Friday, 27 July, 1984

Late this afternoon at around five-thirty Amma expressed a desire to go to the seashore with the Ashramites and visiting devotees. After several days of rain and gray skies, the setting sun's golden rays broke through the clouds as the group led by Amma reached the water's edge. Amma stood looking at the vast ocean and the gigantic waves. As if wanting to touch the Divine Mother's feet, the ocean waves came up to the spot where She was standing. Having washed Her Holy Feet, the waves rolled back to the ocean. As She stood there Amma's bearing reflected Her magnificence. Gently swaying from side to side, Amma kept Her gaze on the horizon. Her eyes were transfixed. The devotees and brahmacharis sat down to meditate, but kept their eyes open and fixed their gaze on the swaying figure of Amma.

Various types of trawlers were lined up on the seashore, as the fishermen had been prevented by the heavy rains from casting their nets out to sea. 'Mother Sea' had not blessed them with a good catch for a long time, except that one day when Amma had helped them. The fishing nets, laid out on the sand to dry, were being gathered up by the men.

Remaining in the same spot, Amma was blissfully enjoying the infinitude. Her dark, curly hair danced in the ocean breeze. Amma's dangling white head scarf looked like a patch of white cloud floating in the sky. The movement of Her body stopped, and She remained motionless, Her eyes wide open. She was totally in an indrawn state.

The sun slowly started its descent into the ocean. With more than half of its fiery orb still visible, it beautified the entire horizon with its golden rays. Eventually the sun disappeared from sight as it dived deep into the ocean waters. As the time approached quarter past six, the translucent veil of dusk spread itself all around. The noisy fisher-children who were somersaulting at the shoreline stopped their play and retreated to their homes, small huts made of thatched coconut leaves and bamboo poles. The constant roar of the endless ocean evoked a feeling of terrifying yet inspiring awe. As this sunny day came to a close, rain clouds slowly filled the entire sky, adding drama to the twilight.

Amma still stood unmoving. It was now more than forty minutes since She had come to the water's edge. Her white head scarf still floated in the breeze, but other than that there was no movement. Concerned, Gayatri and Br. Rao approached Her to make sure all was well. Sensitive to Mother's states of samadhi, they were a bit uncertain and confused about what to do, for rain was impending. Already someone held an umbrella above Amma. Obviously moved by the beauty and the tension of the scene, Br. Pai began to sing slokas by Sri Sankaracharya

> *No desire for Liberation have I,*
> *nor for wealth and knowledge do I crave,*
> *neither do I desire happiness,*
> *O You Moon-faced One;*
> *but this much I beg of You, O Mother,*
> *that my life may be spent chanting Your names.*
>
> *O Mother of the universe,*
> *nothing is there to be wondered*
> *that You should be full of compassion for me,*
> *for a mother does not forsake her son*
> *even if he has numerable faults.*

Transcending the sound of the ocean waves, the song echoed through the twilight. Some fishermen came out of their huts to see what was going on, but as they were familiar with such happenings around Mother, most of them soon disappeared back into their huts though a few stood around as onlookers.

The song was not sung in vain; it served its purpose. After a while, there was a slight movement in Amma's body. First the fingers of Her right hand moved, then there was the peculiar but familiar sound which Amma sometimes makes when She comes out of samadhi. Hearing that, everyone sighed with relief. After a few more moments, Amma completely regained Her regular consciousness.

It was nearly seven o'clock when Amma and the group returned to the Ashram. A few brahmacharis who had stayed behind in the Ashram had already begun the evening bhajan.

Chapter 8

Monday, 30 July, 1984

It was a quiet afternoon. The Ashram looked almost deserted as all were in their own rooms reading, writing or tending to personal matters. Br. Balu was sitting on the temple verandah talking to a middle-aged man who had come from the eastern part of Kerala. The man, Mr. S., was telling Balu how Amma had cured his cancer.

Mr. S. had been suffering from intestinal cancer for the last four years. From the day it was diagnosed he had undergone different treatments, both allopathic and ayurvedic. In spite of all the treatments and medication, the disease persisted. He had intense, unbearable pain in the stomach which had caused him many sleepless nights. Though Mr. S. belonged to a poor family, he received good medical treatment through the help and financial assistance provided by generous friends and doctors. The doctors did their best, but Mr. S. did not get any better. As time passed, his condition worsened. Finally the doctors gave up all hope and advised him to stop all medication. Counting his last days, Mr. S. still did not give up his faith in God. He prayed and chanted almost every day.

Finally one day, assisted by his only brother and his wife, Mr. S. came to see Amma for the first time. During Devi Bhava when Amma asked about his disease, Mr. S. told Her about his incurable illness and prayed to Her to do as She wished. Amma gave him a drink of sacred water from the kindi after She had blessed it by taking a sip Herself. In addition to that Amma gave him some sacred water to take home, instructing him to have a little of it everyday.

"From that day onwards, I started feeling much more relaxed and comfortable. The pain lessened and in a short period of time it was completely gone. I was able to start eating properly and at night I could sleep soundly. Now I am perfectly well. It is almost one year now and still I continue to take Amma's sacred water everyday. I always have a supply of it in my puja room. Amma has blessed me with a second birth. This life belongs to Her."

Mr. S. had wanted Amma's will to be done. He did not ask for a cure. He made no demands. Even when Amma asked him about his illness, the man did not suggest anything to Her. He just prayed, "Let Amma's will be done." That was real prayer. Real prayer is when we pray without ego. The ego should be kept away, for only then are real prayers possible. Mr. S. expressed a real prayer and it was answered. Real prayers must be answered.

Amma says, "A real prayer will never contain any suggestions, instructions or demands. The sincere devotee will simply say, 'O Lord, I do not know what is good or what is bad for me. I am nobody—nothing. You know everything. I know whatever you do must be for the best; therefore, do as you wish.' In real prayer you bow down, surrender and declare your helplessness to the Lord."

While Mr. S. sat on the temple verandah, waiting to have Amma's darshan, She happened to pass by. He rushed to Her and prostrated. Amma affectionately lifted him up and inquired about his health and family. The man was overwhelmed with joy. In an excited mood he replied, "Amma, how can there be any problems when You are guiding me both within and without?"

Surrendering

After spending a few minutes with Mr. S., Amma stepped into the kitchen. The brahmacharinis and women devotees who worked there did not expect this sudden visit. Of course, Amma's visits always happened like this, and the women were quite sure that, as usual, they would be caught for some negligence or other. They waited in fear as Amma looked around. But much to their surprise, Amma simply sat down on the floor. She picked up a cucumber from the corner where the vegetables were stored and started eating it. After having taken a couple of bites, Amma gave it to one of the women devotees who received it joyfully. Others probably felt a twinge of jealousy.

Amma often does things like this when all the residents are around Her. Then She watches everyone's expression and mental attitude to see if some negative feelings are cropping up in anyone's mind. If there are any people feeling jealous, She immediately catches them.

It seemed as if the women devotees were celebrating, for there were only smiling faces on this day. All of them were happy and thrilled. They usually complain that they always have to work, that they have given up everything to be constantly in Amma's presence, but instead they spend half their time in the kitchen cooking, sweating and toiling.

All the kitchen workers now sat around Amma. She started singing Radhe Govinda, and everybody sang the response. Amma, surrounded by all the women and girls, reminded one of Krishna surrounded by the gopis of Vrindavan. This was followed by another song

Ellam ariyunna

No need is there to tell anything
to all-knowing Krishna.
Walking beside us, He sees
and understands everything.

The Primordial Being sees all the thoughts
of the Innermost Self.
It is never possible for anyone to do anything,
forgetting Him.

The Primordial Lord abides in all.
All of us should worship with joy
that Embodiment of Truth and Awareness.

After the songs Amma sat in the middle laughing and cracking jokes. Then the mood changed to a more serious tone.

Amma said, "Mother knows that you sometimes complain about the work load in the kitchen. Children, spirituality is nothing but giving up our happiness whole-heartedly for the sake of others. There shouldn't be any bad feelings or complaints about that. Usually when people give up something they experience a lot of conflict within. They start having second thoughts about it and feel that perhaps they made a mistake. This is not real renunciation. After having given up something, if you still feel a mental attachment to it, that means you have not given it up.

"In fact, what you should give up is the attachment to the object. You can have the object and enjoy it—if you are not attached. We give up something externally, in order to be internally free from the bondage to that object. Detachment is what brings peace and happiness. Real renunciation and detachment come only when we give up all thoughts and feelings about whatever we have renounced.

"Mother has seen many people who still feel very sad and frustrated about something which they gave up long ago. With a voice full of disappointment years later, a person like this says, 'What a fool was I to give that thing away.' Though he has not seen it for years, such a person still carries the burden of the object. He is not free from it even though he has not seen it for many years. Internally he is still attached and bound. This kind of person cannot experience the joy of freedom. He can never feel relaxed. When he still had the object, he did not feel any mental agony. He enjoyed having it. The thought that it was his own made him a happy man. But now he experiences terrible agony, 'I should not have done it. I should never have given it away.' He repeats this over and over again in his mind a hundred times a day.

"Give up something and feel happy about it. Forget that it was ever yours. To think that you have given up something is also wrong. Don't feel that. Just feel relaxed; be at ease. Realize that you are free—free from that burden. The object was a burden and now it is gone. Only if you can feel the burden of attachment to objects will you be able to feel the relaxation or bliss that comes with detachment and renunciation.

"Children, it is true that you have given up your belongings and homes to come and spend the rest of your lives with Amma. But have you really given them up? You still say, 'We have given up everything to be in Amma's physical presence, but just as we did at home, we are still working in the kitchen.' This means you have not given them up because it sounds as if you are disappointed about having done so. You still carry the thought, 'We have given up our house and everything.' This constant thought makes it very clear that you still carry the house and all the household utensils within you.

"Children, try to feel relaxed and at ease about it. Try to feel that you have unburdened yourselves of a heavy load, and now feel happy about doing this work here because you are not doing it for yourselves. You are serving all those who come here. They are devotees of God. You are the ones who cook food for them, food which gives them both physical and mental strength to remember God. This is a great service that you are doing. By serving devotees of God, you are serving God. Consider this work as a sadhana."

A brahmacharini asked, "It is said that a spiritual person should not even expect a word of thanks or gratitude for the service that he or she does. Amma, what does that mean?"

"That is right," replied Amma. "A true seeker should not expect even one word of appreciation. Suppose we do some service for someone. We complete it beautifully. Then the person for whom we have done the work comes along with his friends and relatives to see it. They like it very much; they appreciate it, and praise the quality of the work that we have done. They express their gratitude using flowery words. When all this happens, when they shower you with praises and words of thanks, you remain humble. You may even say, 'Oh for heaven's sake, don't say this. I don't deserve all these praises. I am just a tool. He, the Supreme Being, does everything through me. Without His grace I am nothing. Please bow down to Him. Shower all these praises on Him. He is the real doer, not I.' But these words are superficial; they don't come from deep within. You are not really humble. You just pretend to be humble. You put up a big show of humility. It is simple psychology. You want others to think that you are a humble devotee devoid of all egoistic feelings. But in reality, all the praises and flowery words they have spoken go to your head and you start feeling proud. 'I am not an ordinary soul,' you think. 'There must be something special about me; otherwise, how could I do this work so well? Look at all these people praising me and my talents. I must really be great.' In this way, thought after thought goes to boost the ego.

"Even a simple word of thanks can work in this way. It enters into your head and makes you feel that you are something special. As sadhaks we are striving hard to feel that we are nothing and that He is everything. But such circumstances work on us very subtly. Without even knowing it, we can become bound by words of thanks and praise. Therefore, if you wish to help someone, fine. Do so, but do not feel that others should thank you or praise you for anything you have done.

"It has become our habit to expect something in return for our help, a single word of gratitude or a sentence of praise like 'You have done wonderful work. We really appreciate it.' And that's enough to make you feel a bit of pride. That's enough for you to get the feeling that you have really done something wonderful. Even the thought, 'I did it,' is food for your ego. When the ego is fed, it feels great.

"When we donate or offer something to a temple, church, or a spiritual institution, we sincerely wish that others could know about it. We wait for some recognition or thanks. We want acknowledgment for our great grand offering. We want someone to say in public that this generous, open-hearted philanthropist has done something great, something wonderful for society. Without praise, we don't feel satisfied.

"There is a story of a great Mahatma who worked as a priest in a temple. He was a fully surrendered soul. There was not a trace of ego in him. One day a multi-millionaire donated a huge sum of money to the temple. Afterwards, the rich man kept on speaking to the priest about the tremendous amount of money that he had donated. He said that even for a multi-millionaire like him the amount was huge. Over and over he repeated the same thing. The Mahatma kept quiet for some time. But when he found that the rich man was not going to stop, the Mahatma asked, 'Okay, sir, what do you want? Do you expect something? Something in return? A word of praise or a word of thanks?' The

195

rich man replied, 'What is wrong with that? I can expect at least that much.' The Mahatma smilingly looked at him and said, 'If so, take this money back. We do not want it here. You should be thankful to the Lord for accepting this amount. You should feel content, thinking that you could return at least a portion of the wealth that the Great Lord has entrusted to you. You should be thankful to God, for He gave you an opportunity to serve Him. If you cannot do that, please take this money back.'

"Children, that should be our attitude. Who are we, the debtors, to demand or expect something from Him? Our giving is nothing but remitting. We cannot give anything to Him. We can only make a remittance of what we owe God. We call it giving, but that is wrong. To become spiritual, to become egoless, which is our goal in life, we should be able to feel thankful to Him for everything. Never let 'I' come in. Let there be only 'You,' the attitude that everything is 'You.' Never ask for anything, never demand anything. Let Him decide what to give and what not to give."

"Children, this opportunity you have, to work and serve the devotees and sadhaks, should be considered a rare gift bestowed upon you by the Lord to quickly exhaust your prarabdha or accumulated tendencies. Cooking food and serving the devotees of God is no small thing. It is a rare blessing. You are really the blessed ones in the Ashram. When you were in your own homes, you were only preparing food for your husbands and your children, for a small family of five or six. There is nothing great in cooking with love for one's own family. But cooking for others with love and dedication is an act of greatness. This will definitely purify you, uplift you and finally take you to the goal. You should be thankful to God to be given such an opportunity for having been chosen to work in the kitchen. Wherever your work be—in the kitchen, the cow shed or the toilet—let that be your temple. Make your workplace your place of worship, the place where you do your sadhana. Do not curse your work. Feel happy and blessed, and perform your work whole-heartedly."

All of a sudden Amma's mood changed. The Great Teacher who vigorously expounded the highest Truth with unchallengeable authority was gone, and in it's place was a playful and innocent two-year-old child. Amma lay down on the bare kitchen floor, placing Her head on a woman's lap and Her feet on another's. Quite unexpectedly, Amma said, "Where is my cucumber? I want my cucumber." But it was gone! Indeed, who could resist eating Amma's prasad? Someone quickly fetched another one and offered it to Amma. She looked at it but soon pushed it away like a stubborn child saying, "No, I don't want this one. I want mine, the one I was eating."

Falling under the spell of Amma's childlike mood, some older devotees acted exactly like mothers who were really concerned about their child. They tried to coax Amma to accept the new cucumber but failed. Others were thrilled, enjoying the whole scene with great devotion. Amma whimpered like a child and repeatedly asked for the same cucumber from which She had taken a few bites. Finally when Amma did not get it, She pulled the devotee who had eaten it by her hair. In that position, still holding the woman's hair, Amma went into samadhi. After some time Amma got up and left the kitchen. She entered the temple and closed the door. Amma remained inside the temple almost for an hour.

Referring to Herself, Amma once said, "Something—an object, a desire or a thought—is needed to keep the mind down on this physical plane. Otherwise, it is difficult to stop it from shooting up. When the body expresses a desire, that is what it is for." The cucumber business might have been one such play.

Chapter 9

All the residents of the Ashram participated in the large scale cleaning that began at ten o'clock in the morning. Of course, when Amma is there to work along with the group, there is no question of anybody not joining in. On such occasions, everybody's energy is high, for in Amma's presence, it is easy to feel the joy of selfless action. To work alongside Amma is a wonderful experience. Radiating spiritual light and energy, She actively participates in all the Ashram work. Amma never fails to inspire the residents, whatever kind of work they do.

That particular morning all the residents were working hard, blissfully chanting the Divine Names, feeling great enthusiasm and vigor as they worked. Amma sang too and did the work with immense joy. All together they sang

Adbhuta Charite

O You to whom the celestials bow
Whose tale is wonderful,
Grant us the strength to be devoted to Your Feet.

We offer You all our actions
Done in the darkness of ignorance.
O Protector of the distressed,

Forgive us for all impertinent utterances,
O Ruler of the Universe.

O Mother, please shine in my heart
Like the rising sun at dawn.
Give me a mind of equal vision
Free of a differentiating intellect.

O Great Goddess, Cause of all actions
Both sinful and virtuous,
O Liberator from all bondage,
Give me Your sandals which protect the basic virtues
On the path of Liberation,
The essence of all Principles.

It seemed as though Amma was everywhere. She was seen at one place sweeping, at another place carrying sand and brick, at still another place chopping wood, or removing dirt in yet another place.

Do not think that the world will change after one attains Self-realization. Outwardly everything remains the same. Nothing really changes. The trees, the mountains, the valleys, the rivers and streams, the birds singing on the branches of trees—everything remains unchanged. The world will move on its own. But indescribable change happens within. Your entire being is transformed. You see things differently with an entirely new eye. There will be an inexplicable quality in you and in the work you do. A constant stream of aesthetic delight springs forth from within you. Just like an innocent child you wonder at everything you behold.

If one closely observes Amma one can clearly see this quality in Her. There is a special beauty in whatever work She does. That beauty can be perceived in all Her actions, in all Her movements. She does the same work as others, but the way Amma does it is so charming and enrapturing to the heart. Amma does it with the delight and wonder of an innocent child, and that childlike innocence encompasses us. That fullness of Love in which She is established can be perceived in everything Amma does.

The work was almost completed. Amma sat down on the sand and asked Gayatri to bring some coffee and some snacks for everyone. Gayatri headed toward the kitchen. Usually after group work like this, Amma likes to serve something hot to drink and to distribute something light, like banana chips, to everyone as prasad.

Amma raised both Her hands and called out, "Hey, Shivane!" Then Amma remarked, "That 'old man' is mindless! He doesn't care about anything." Everybody laughed delightedly.

Spirituality is real wealth

Taking this as a good opportunity to clarify a question he had, one of the residents asked, "Amma, there are different versions of what spirituality is. It is said that stillness of mind is spirituality or that spirituality is a state of silence. Renunciation of desires and desire-prompted actions is spirituality. Expansiveness of mind is real spirituality. These, and so many more different views exist about spirituality. Amma what do you say about this?"

Amma answered, "Spirituality is everything that you have mentioned. It is stillness of mind, a state of silence. It is also renunciation or an egoless state. Stillness is something to be experienced. Everything you have mentioned has to be experienced. You can write volumes about spirituality. You can compose beautiful poetry about it and sing about it in melodious songs. You can also speak about spirituality for hours in very beautiful and flowery language. But still spirituality will remain unknown to you unless you really experience its beauty and bliss from within.

"Children, spirituality is the real wealth. Spirituality is the inner wealth which helps one to renounce all outer wealth, through an understanding of the meaninglessness of external riches. It is the wealth which helps one to become 'wealthier than the wealthiest.' It is the realization that God alone, the Self alone, is the real wealth. Spirituality is the wealth that helps us have a healthy approach to life."

Amma stopped for a while and continued by telling a story.

"A villager once had a dream. Lord Shiva appeared before him in this dream and said, 'Tomorrow at daybreak go to the outskirts of the village. There you will find a sannyasin. Ask him for the precious stone that will make you a rich man forever.' That night the man couldn't sleep, for he was always thinking of the precious stone he was going to get. Finally, in the morning as instructed by Lord Shiva in the dream, he rushed to the outskirts of the village. There he was overwhelmed to actually find a sannyasin who just arrived. The latter was about to settle down under a tree when the villager came running up to him saying, 'Where is the stone, the precious stone? Give me the precious stone.' The sannyasin looked up and asked, 'What did you say? A precious stone!' Without uttering another word, he opened a bundle lying next to him and took out a large precious gem. The sannyasin handed it over to the villager without hesitation.

"The villager looked and looked, and again looked at the stone. He was wonder struck because it was a diamond, probably the biggest in the world. With a joyful heart full of hopes and wishes, the man returned home. But that night again he could not sleep. He tossed about in bed. The next morning before dawn the villager once again rushed to the outskirts of the village. He woke the sannyasin and said, 'Be kind enough to bestow on me the wealth which made you give this diamond to me so easily.'

"Children, once you know your essential nature, the entire universe becomes your wealth. In that supreme state you have nothing to gain or lose. Having given up all attachment you become ever established in the state of supreme detachment. Just like the sannyasin in the story, you can smilingly give up even so-called precious objects and still feel content and peaceful. Spirituality is inner wealth which makes you feel fully content. You may have nothing to claim as your own, but you can still be full and content. Once you attain that state, you have nothing else to gain or lose. Once you acquire that inner spiritual wealth, you start living in fullness. Externally you may not be wealthy at all, but internally you are rich and full. You realize that you are the master of the entire universe. You become the master of water, air, earth, and ether, sun, moon, stars and space. Everything in the universe will be under your control. Therefore, children, try to become a master, not a slave.

"A real wealthy man is one who can always smile, even in the face of sorrow. Sorrow cannot make him cry nor does he need happiness to make him rejoice. He does not need the support of objects or favorable external events in order to be happy. By his very nature he is blissful. An externally rich man is a miserable man who does not really know what real happiness is. In this regard he is a loser, even without knowing it. He always loses the priceless wealth—that is, peace and contentment."

As Mother was talking, Gayatri arrived with the coffee and banana chips. As Amma passed out prasad to Her children, She asked the brahmacharis to sing

Bandhamilla

No one is ours
There is nothing to call our own,
In our last days only the True Self
Will remain as ours.

We take nothing with us on the last journey
Why then this madness for earthly possessions?

That which truly exists is within us
To see That, we must go within.

There no trace of sorrow exists
There the True Self shines in Its own glory.
We go from untruth to Truth
When we love and serve all living beings.

Chapter 10

Necessity of the Guru's grace

Tuesday, 7 August, 1984

On the southwestern corner of the Ashram just behind the water tank grew some sugarcane. In the afternoon Amma cut a fresh stalk and began eating it. Just like a child who delights in sucking the juice from the sugarcane, Amma relished it with great pleasure. A few brahmacharis and a woman devotee from the neighborhood were sitting next to Her.

Anyone who sees Amma apparently relishing a particular food or drink naturally feels that She has a special liking for it. Always wishing to please Her, later they will prepare this same food or keep a stock of it on hand in case they should have the chance to offer some to Her. But often what Amma seems to like so much on one occasion, She will never ask for again.

Once Amma kept asking adamantly for 'mixture,' a spicy combination of different bits of deep-fried bakery items. Br. Nealu had a small quantity of it, and he offered that to Amma. She took the tin container from Nealu and spread the mixture all over the cement floor. Then She started to eat the pieces off the floor, crawling around like a little child. As Nealu and Br. Balu happily witnessed this scene, they thought Amma would love to have more of it, and decided it would be a good idea to keep a stock of 'mixture' on hand, so they could readily offer it to Amma whenever She asked. So they purchased some and kept it safely for Her. But they were disappointed because Amma never asked for 'mixture' again. Amma calls this play of Hers "a totally detached attachment to keep the mind down."

Some devotees who were sincere sadhaks were visiting the Ashram from Tamil Nadu. They stood at a respectful distance watching Amma eating the sugarcane. She called them near. Without hesitation they rushed to Amma, prostrated at Her feet and sat down. One of them who was madly in love with Amma wanted to sit as close as he could to Her. Although he was nearly sixty, the man acted like a three-year-old child in Her presence.

Amma gave a piece of sugarcane to everyone, including the brahmacharis. It was always so special to receive prasad from Amma's hands. One could never get too much of it. Whether it was sugarcane or a ball of rice, whatever one received was an indescribable blessing.

"Amma, I have read that no matter how much sadhana one does, the state of Perfection cannot be reached without the grace of a Satguru. Is this true?" asked one of the Tamil devotees.

She answered, "Perfectly correct. In order to remove the subtler vasanas one needs the Guru's guidance and grace. Again, when the vasanas are removed, the last stage, the point when a sadhak falls or glides into the state of Perfection, cannot happen without his grace.

"Human beings are limited. They cannot do much on their own. Maybe they are able to proceed to a certain stage without anybody's guidance or help, but soon the way becomes complex and help is required. The road to liberation is a maze of intricate paths, a labyrinth. In traveling through the maze, a spiritual aspirant may not be able to figure out where to go or which way to turn.

"Or following a spiritual path without a Guru can be compared to sailing alone in the ocean in a tiny boat that is not equipped with the necessary equipment, not even a compass to indicate the direction.

"Remember that the path which leads to the state of Self-realization is very narrow. Two people cannot walk together hand in hand rubbing each other's shoulders in companionship along this path. One walks this path alone.

"As we walk on the spiritual path there is a light that guides us. That light, showing us the path, is the Guru's grace. The Guru walks in front shedding light on the path as he slowly and carefully leads us. He knows all the intricate paths by heart. The light of his grace helps us to see and remove the obstacles and reach the ultimate goal.

"Children, only out of compassion does the Guru come down to walk with us. As we slowly walk behind him, we follow in the light of his grace. It is his grace which protects us and saves us from falling down. The Guru's grace helps us not to get lost in the darkness of narrow lanes and slip into dangerous pitfalls.

"Sometimes the path becomes very narrow. If it becomes too narrow and you slip off the path, it is necessary to have a Guru pull you back on. Otherwise, left to your own devices, you may retrace your steps and you may find it too difficult, almost impossible, to continue on the right way. In such places too, the Guru encourages you; he instills more faith and confidence in you to try again and again. Without the Guru's encouraging and inspiring words, without his loving and compassionate glances, and without the faith and courage he instills in you, you might not even try. You cannot cross the final barrier by your own effort alone. Your effort is nothing. From the other side where he dwells, the Guru extends his hand and pulls you through.

"Without the Guru you may turn back and stray from the path. It is quite possible for you to get entangled in the world again. Feeling discouraged and disillusioned, you may even proclaim to the world that spirituality is not a reality, that it is a myth, an illusion. These and other dangerous ideas may take root in your mind.

"In reality, the Guru's pushing and pulling is not pushing and pulling, that is, you are pushed and pulled without being pushed and pulled. You do not feel it because his compassion and love envelop you totally, so you don't feel that you are being pushed and pulled. You don't feel pressure, stress or strain. But if his grace and guidance were not present, the stress and pressure of your own vasanas would cause you to stray from the path of spirituality.

"Some places are broad, flooded with light, where the atmosphere is filled with divine fragrance. Your own mind will try to delude you by creating a colorful world. There will be attractive, tempting and alluring sights all around—divine music on one side, enchanting dances on the other. It may look like the final goal. You may feel this is the final goal and therefore you may stop. Not wanting to proceed further, you won't feel like moving. It is like a 'mini-liberation state,' a kind of imitation. You may even feel that you have reached the goal, that you have attained Realization.

"When you think that you have attained Realization, the very worst will start happening. Slowly and furtively the ego will enter. You won't see him coming in. You won't recognize him, and even if you do recognize him, you won't care because you will be so enamored of the idea that you are truly realized. Thus you will try to overlook his trickery. Or you may feel, 'This is how it is after Realization.' So you start enjoying old habits and indulging in old pleasures, and so you fall back into the world.

"Children, you don't have any idea about how life will be after Realization because you are not realized. As far as you are concerned, the state is totally unknown. You are simply assuming that you are realized, but there is no ground for this assumption. A sadhak who makes this assumption, who feels he is already realized, is wrong. There are no feelings in that state. Even the thought 'I have reached' will not exist. However, if you feel this, then that is another thought which will block your path. You have not yet attained the state of Perfection, for Truth is far beyond. But to convince you of this, to show you the Truth, a Satguru is needed. The Guru's grace is absolutely necessary.

"The Guru knows all there is to know. He knows that what you see and what you hear are just illusions. He makes you understand this so that you do not get trapped thinking that what you perceive is reality. He constantly encourages and inspires you to go further and further beyond the jungles of illusion until you reach the shore of enlightenment.

"Along the spiritual journey, there will come a time when your growth becomes spontaneous. You may not know that you are growing within, but the Guru will know. To reach this stage of spontaneous growth requires much self-effort. It is like shooting a rocket into space. A lot of human effort and fuel is needed to shoot a rocket beyond the earth's gravity. Once it is beyond the gravitational force of the earth the upward movement becomes automatic, and then it can go into the orbit of another planet.

"Likewise, the sadhak needs to put forth a great amount of self-effort until he reaches the stage of spontaneous growth. Once he enters that stage, inner transformation will happen effortlessly, even without his own knowledge. But the Guru knows because it is he who has taken the sadhak into that realm. It is the Guru who showered the grace on him to take the final leap.

"The final push into that stage of spontaneous growth cannot happen without the help of the Guru. He is the only one who knows that spontaneous growth is taking place and that the final attainment will be achieved soon. He knows that his grace is already flowing toward the sadhak and that it will bear fruit without much delay. For the sadhak, this period may be like a waiting period because he is not aware of the inner transformation that is taking place. He does not know that the Guru has bestowed his grace upon him. As far as the sadhak is concerned, this is a time when all conscious effort stops. He can do nothing but wait. Then all of a sudden, it happens, the inner awakening. Even without his own knowledge, the grace bestowed by the Guru takes him there. Out of nowhere it happens. Grace comes out of nowhere. It can happen at anytime, at any place.

"The Satguru's grace is what's needed the most. Without his loving care, compassionate glances and affectionate touch, one cannot reach the goal. With each compassionate glance and touch, he is sending forth his grace. Therefore, children, pray for his grace."

It was time for the Tamil devotees to leave. One by one they went up to Amma and prostrated. The devotee who was madly devoted to Amma chanted a Tamil verse glorifying the Divine Mother. It was a poem by a poet named Maanikkavaachakar:

> You bestowed on me a grace undeserved
> and enabled this slave's body and soul
> to joyfully thaw and melt with love.
> For this I have nothing to give in return,
> O Emancipator pervading the past,
> the future and every thing!
> O Infinite Primal Being...

When he had finished the verse, he prostrated at Her Feet. Amma expressed Her love and concern for each one of the Tamil devotees in a very distinct way. When one of the devotees was about to touch Amma's feet, She caught hold of both his hands and told him in a voice full of authority, "Tell your teacher that if it is his view that all old concepts of spirituality should die, he should not even study the scriptures because those are all old concepts written by the ancient rishis, aren't they? Remind him that by asking people not to follow a Guru he himself is becoming a Guru. Also ask him to be humble. Tell him that he is trying to hear music only by placing the sheet music to his ears. He is like one who is trying to bathe or swim in a picture of a river."

Hearing Amma's words, the Tamil devotee was stunned. There was an obvious look of wonder on his face. Amma still held both his hands. All of a sudden, the devotee burst into tears, placing Amma's hands on his face. Amma sat with a mischievous smile on Her face. The devotee remained in that position for some time and kept crying. At last Amma consoled him saying, "Don't worry. Amma was simply joking. Don't take it seriously."

The devotee now raised his head and said, "No, no. You are not joking. Why do you say that? Now after meeting you and hearing these words directly from you, how can I believe that you are joking? No, you cannot be joking. What you said is the truth. He is very egotistic. But my firm conviction is that he will be humbled when he hears your remarks." Amma smiled. There was hidden meaning in Her smile.

Before the Tamil devotee left the Ashram, one of the brahmacharis who was curious to know more about that incident, approached the devotee and expressed his wish to him. This is what he told him.

The Tamil devotee had a teacher who taught him the scriptures. This man had a lot of bookish knowledge and thought very highly of himself and of his ability to teach spirituality through the scriptures. His dictum was, "Study of the scriptures is enough. Meditation and devotional singing and other spiritual practices are not of much use. They are all old concepts. It is high time to die to the old and have a new vision of spirituality." He was also opposed to following a Guru. When this man heard that his student was going to see a great saint in Kerala, his doubting and argumentative mind started functioning. He summoned his student and said, "I have heard that you were going to have the darshan of a so-called 'great saint' in Kerala. I have also heard that She is all-knowing, that She knows the past, present and future. Of course, I do not believe that. But still, if this is true, let Her prove Her omniscience. Let Her give me a sign, a message or something to prove that She is all-knowing. If She does that, I too will go to see Her."

So when this devotee who was a student of that scholar was about to leave after having sat in Amma's presence, he felt some disappointment. Though his personal experience with Amma was very elevating, She had not said one word or even given a hint about his teacher, who was anxiously waiting for proof. At last, when Amma finally disclosed it at such an unexpected moment, he was stunned and grateful at the same time and could not control his emotions. Tears still welled up in his eyes as he was leaving the Ashram.

Amma's remarks hit the target. After receiving the proof he had asked for, the scholar came to Amma. Even though he himself had a number of admirers and followers, the man became a devotee of Amma.

A Guru's warning

When the Tamil devotee left, Amma called one of the brahmacharis and scolded him for his disobedience. One of the elder brahmacharis had asked him to do a particular job, but he simply refused. When the elder asked why, the younger replied, "I have no time. There is no other explanation for it." The elder brahmachari reported this matter to Amma, and now the one at fault was being scolded. In being scolded by Amma, one also gets some good advice. As Amma was talking to him, pointing out his errors, She said, "You are very egotistic."

This brahmachari was occasionally very stubborn and argumentative. He retorted, "Then why did you take me as a brahmachari if you knew that I was very egotistic?"

Amma's compassionate answer flowed, "Why did Jesus Christ accept Judas as His disciple? Didn't He know that Judas was going to betray Him, that he was going to lead Him to His death? Yes, Jesus knew that very well. Nevertheless, Jesus accepted Judas as one of His disciples. He loved him just as He loved the others.

"Didn't the great saints and sages of the past consciously give opportunities to those who cheated them later? Mahatmas are like that. They cannot be otherwise. They don't think about or care whether somebody will cheat them or love them or whether someone will be egoistic. They don't expect anything from anyone. They are just there. Anybody who is willing, who is ready to open his or her heart, and who is ready to surrender, can benefit from their presence. Opportunities are open to everyone. Mahatmas don't differentiate. They cannot do that. Even if someone is a cheat or is very egoistic, if he or she surrenders only for a few days or a few minutes—the time does not matter—their surrender for that much time will have its benefit.

"After that, if the person withdraws himself, what can the Mahatma do? The Mahatma cannot do anything. He simply is. If you want him, he is available—all the time, everywhere. If you do not want him, he is still there available to anyone else. But if you reject him, he cannot force himself on you. That is one thing he cannot do.

"However, if you surrender, he will flow into your heart. When only a small portion of your heart is filled with the Guru, the larger, unfilled portion will still be under the influence of the ego saying, 'I am something.' That small filled portion will still remain. It will work. That part of you will have its power. That part will try to save you. You will feel it. But remember now, it is only a little filled while a big portion remains unfilled. That bigger portion is filled with 'I am something.'

"Children, the danger comes when you totally neglect the small filled portion, not even looking toward that side. If you can throw a glance to that side, the side where the Guru is, you will still have hope. You can still be saved. But the ego, which covers the bigger portion, completely neglects him. The Guru will warn you, not once, but a hundred times he'll instruct you and give hints to you. But if you completely shut the door, if you bang the door right in his face, what can he do? Then the pressure or the pull of 'I am something' becomes stronger in you, and you naturally move to that side. Of course, that is easier. To move to the Guru's side needs a little more effort, a little more courage.

"The government and the university provide equal opportunities to all students, but the students utilize these opportunities differently. The same analogy can be made about people who desire spirituality. Many are interested in spirituality, but only a few will 'make the grade,' so to speak. Merely being interested is not sufficient. Intensity is what is needed. It is not the Guru's fault. A Satguru cannot be wrong. He can only be right. You are wrong. We are like a musical instrument that is off-key. The Guru wants to repair the keys that are off. But if you protest, if you strongly feel you are all right, if you think there is no problem with you, that the 'off key' is all right because you don't hear it as being 'off,' then what can the Guru do? In order to make the keys sound more pleasant to the ears, a little scratching, scrubbing, scraping and removing is needed. You should be able to bear the pain caused by this, understanding its purpose is to make your life harmonious, as in a musical concert.

"Amma is crazy, but Her craziness is for Truth and dharma. If somebody moves against Truth, if he is not at all ready to mend his ways, if he is determined to do things his own way, then he is going away from Amma. He is moving away from Truth and dharma. Remember, Amma is not going away from him; She cannot. But he, through his own actions and thoughts, is creating a gulf between Amma and him. Once that happens, the gap becomes wider and wider.

"Amma cannot accept or reject anyone. Acceptance and rejection are possible only when there is ego. The ego can accept and reject. When one becomes egoless, one goes beyond both. Therefore, it is you who accept and reject. Amma cannot. However, there is one thing that you should keep in mind. Your goal is to reach the state of Perfection. Now the question is whether you really want it or not. Sometimes 'yes' and sometimes 'no' is out of the question. If this is your attitude, then this is not your place. There is no such thing as vacillation in spirituality. There is either 'yes' or 'no.' That is it. If you feel spiritual sometimes and non-spiritual at other times, that is not spirituality. What Amma means is that your mind should be fixed on That, i.e., the goal. There ought to be no distractions. It is dangerous if you simply let yourself be carried away by circumstantial distractions. Since your main purpose in life is to realize God, the awareness of the goal and intent to reach it, otherwise known as lakshya bodha, should always be present.

"Suppose you are an executive. When you sit in your chair at the office, your entire thought process should be focused on how to manage the company—how to make more profit, how to solve the employees' problems and how to create a good market for your products. That is your dharma while you are at the office. You are not supposed to be thinking about your family and its problems at that time. That is your dharma when you are at home. If you think about your home while sitting in the office, then the whole purpose of your job as an executive is not being carried out properly. And vice versa, if you think and act like a executive at home, instead of being a husband and father, you are not fulfilling your duties. Likewise, when you are here in the Ashram as a brahmachari or one who aspires to become a brahmachari, you are supposed to act and think in a certain way. If you cannot have the proper attitude, you won't fit in here. You will start feeling the gulf, the gap which will finally result in a lot of problems in your spiritual life.

"Amma will constantly create circumstances which will help your spiritual growth. She can pardon and forget a hundred times or more. But if you constantly struggle and pull your hands away from Amma's, you cannot blame Her."

Forget the past

Friday, 10 August, 1984

At about eleven o'clock in the morning Amma was sitting on Her cot which was kept outside on the south side of the Ashram. She was surrounded by Western and Indian devotees. A question was raised by one of the Western devotees, "Many people doubt that they can meditate on God and realize Him because they feel they have committed too many sins that will prevent them from God-realization. They feel that they will not receive God's grace."

Amma's reply was immediate, "There is no basis for such doubts and worries. Once determination and detachment arise, the past becomes ineffective. The past loses its grip on a person who has surrendered everything at the Feet of the Lord. Such a person glides into a forgetful state about his entire past, and he starts living in the beautiful present where he sees only the Lord and His Enchanting Form. The fearful dreams about the past completely die in a surrendered soul, and he will definitely feel God's grace guiding him throughout.

"Amma will tell you a story to illustrate how the Lord's grace is absolutely available for everyone, even for people who have committed serious errors.

"One night a notorious thief was scouting about to find a suitable house to burglarize. As he furtively walked down the road unnoticed by anyone, he saw a gathering by the roadside of people listening intently to one man who was obviously a story-teller. This storyteller was narrating the childhood sports of Lord Krishna as depicted in the Srimad Bhagavatam. The description of Baby Krishna attracted the attention of the thief. The narrator expounded the Child's beauty, 'Thus Yasoda, Krishna's foster mother, after having bathed the endearing Child of Vrindavan, adorned Him, the All-alluring One, with sparkling jewels. Necklaces studded with diamonds, emeralds and rubies graced His neck, and a golden crown embedded with precious gems adorned the Lord's radiant head. Jingling anklets rang like bells on His feet, accompanied by the melodic tinkling of the golden chain encircling His waist. As Yasoda was further enhancing Krishna's already enchanting Form with ornaments, the Child playfully ran away and hid behind a tree. Yasoda ran after the Boy, calling and calling Him with overflowing love and affection, "Kanna, Kanna".' "

As She said the last sentence, Amma became so identified with the narration that She began gesturing with Her hands. It was as if Krishna were standing right in front of Her. Even Her facial expression bore that love and affection which Yasoda had for Child Krishna. At this point, Amma became intoxicated with pure love and sat still. Tears streamed down Her cheeks as She uttered a laugh every now and then. This state continued for some time; then after a while Amma resumed telling the story.

"As the thief was listening to the story, he was suddenly struck with an idea, 'This Child must be a rich man's son. I must somehow find out where this Baby lives. If I can get hold of this Little One, that would be the end of all my troubles. The precious stones and golden jewelry on this Child are enough for my family and me to live on for the rest of our lives.' So he waited until the narration came to its completion and the storyteller packed up to go. The thief followed him cautiously at some distance until they reached a lonely spot when he suddenly jumped upon the storyteller. Holding him by the neck, the thief threatened, 'Tell me where that Child lives. Where is this place called Vrindavan? Don't try to play any tricks. Tell me the truth. Give me the details of how to get to His house or prepare to die.'

"The storyteller was so shocked he could not speak at all. On the further nudging and threats of the thief, he finally said, 'That was only a story. The Child isn't real. It is only a fabricated tale. It is not a real story.' But the thief was not going to give up so easily. 'Speak the truth,' he said, 'I know you're lying. How can you describe the child so precisely if he never existed? Open your mouth and speak or you're going to die.'

"The storyteller tried and tried to convince the thief that the description was only from a story, explaining that the elaborate portrayal was only to entertain people's vivid imagination, that it was not reality. But the thief had no doubts about the existence of

Baby Krishna and was determined to find this Child. At last, the storyteller thought of a place where there were no human beings or houses but only dense forest. Hoping to get rid of the thief, he told him that Krishna dwelled in this remote place, thinking that the thief would become prey to wild animals in that forest. Taking note of the details of how to get there, the thief released the storyteller, giving him a final warning that if he did not find the Child, he would return and put an end to the storyteller's life.

"Proceeding toward the place indicated by the storyteller, the thief walked rapidly with determination for three days, not stopping to eat or sleep. Along the entire way the thief thought of Krishna and the great fortune that he was going to have. Though with a different intention, in fact, an intention of misdemeanor, his mind was nonetheless totally fixed on the Lord's beautiful form. It took a couple of days for him to reach his destination and by the time he reached the forest, he was totally exhausted. Both feet were bleeding, for they had been punctured by thorns and sharp rocks.

"But the thief was still full of hope because the storyteller had told him Krishna would come if a person called to Him. He had also been told that Krishna and his playmates would usually come to that forest with their cows, and they would frolic about, while the cattle grazed. When the thief did not see anyone, he called and called, his voice ringing throughout the forest, 'Krishna! Krishna! Where are you?' Wandering in search of the Child, he looked in the bushes and behind huge trees. He even climbed to the tops of trees in order to get a higher vantage point to see if Krishna were anywhere else in the forest. As he continued to roam the forest calling out 'Krishna,' his search reached a climax of intensity and desperation. Finally, from lack of food and sleep, he collapsed into unconsciousness. Yet even in this unconscious state he continued to murmur Krishna's name.

"Upon regaining normal consciousness, the thief found himself on someone's lap. Someone was holding and stroking his head and a voice said, "You are exhausted. Here, I've brought you some food." He looked up and was astonished to see before him none other than the Child for whom he had been searching. It was Krishna! And he was lying on His lap. He rubbed his eyes and blinked several times; he could not believe what he was seeing. Yes, it was Krishna... there was the peacock feather, the curly hair, the golden crown, the yellow robe adorned with precious jewels. He was captivated by the all-alluring smile and the dark blue complexion of His face. His eyes were transfixed, for he was unable to take them off of Krishna's glorious countenance. As the Child fed him, he automatically opened his mouth and swallowed the food. Oblivious to everything else around him, he languished in bliss.

"Krishna helped him sit up on his own. Next He removed all His ornaments, wrapped them up and handed them in one bundle to the thief, telling him, 'Here, this is yours. This is what you came for, wasn't it. So now you can go. You can return happy.' Still drinking in the eternal beauty of the Lord, the thief was now totally transformed. He chokingly protested, 'No, no! I do not want that. I want You. I want You.' Krishna continued to urge him, 'You should not return empty-handed. You must not be disappointed after such a long search. Take it.' To this the thief replied, 'My dear Krishna, I do not want anything. I want to embrace You. I want to lie on Your lap. I want to look at Your face. I want to be with You forever and forever. Please, Lord. Please...'"

At this point Amma stood up from the cot where She was sitting. Her entire being was transformed into an incomprehensible bhava of Divinity. There was an extraordinary glow and radiance on Her face. The fingers of Her right hand held the chinmudra.

A bewitching smile further enhanced Her already radiant countenance. Someone exclaimed that Amma looked exactly as She did during Krishna Bhava, yet still there was an inexpressible and indescribable feeling about this present state of Hers. Her body gently swayed from side to side, as a constant and very strong vibration could be detected in Her entire body. The devotees felt very blissful and bathed in supreme devotion.

Seeing the Divine ecstatic mood of Amma, the brahmacharis burst into a song

Govardhana Giri

O You who lifted up Govardhana Hill,
Who play in the hearts of the shepherdesses
Who protect Gokula and indulge in play
Who make the sweet sound on the flute.

You have danced on the snake Kaliya's head
In order to dispel fear of him caused by his pride.
O You who destroy desires and offer desired things
Please do not delay in coming even for a moment,
O You with large eyes like lotus petals.

You are the One who gives the fruits
Of one's accumulated actions.
Trying to control the five senses,
My mind shakes like a peacock feather.
O Krishna, when will I merge in Your Feet?

Slowly Amma came back to the physical plane. She still remained standing in the bliss-intoxicated bhava. With faltering steps She moved toward the cot. Drunk with eternal bliss, She looked like one who was completely out of Her body. One of the woman devotees helped Amma sit on the cot. After some time She regained consciousness completely. Reminded by one of the brahmacharis, Amma continued the story.

"All right, where were we... Oh, yes. Krishna dropped the bundle in front of him and disappeared. Mad with love, the thief ran hither and thither, calling out, 'O Krishna, where are You? Don't leave me. Take me with You. My Lord, come back, come back.' "

It was quite obvious that Amma was struggling hard to keep Herself down on the physical plane. Pausing every now and then, Amma continued to tell the story.

"However, Krishna did not reveal His physical form to the thief again. Unable to bear the excruciating pain of separation, the thief wandered and wandered in the forest calling for Krishna. Days passed and he dejectedly retraced his steps home, carefully cherishing the bundle containing the jewelry which belonged to His Lord.

"Still tightly embracing the bundle, he reached the storyteller's house and knocked on the door. Peeping though the window, the storyteller recognized the thief and was frightened. Filled with fear, he was sure the thief had returned to 'finish him off' because he had not found Krishna, the Blue Boy of Vrindavan. As the knocking on the door continued, the trembling of the man in the house increased. But had he listened carefully, he could have heard the thief say in a feeble voice, "I have seen the Lord, my Krishna. I have seen my Lord..." Knowing the fierce reputation of the thief, he was afraid that if he did not open the door, the thief would break it down and kill him anyway. So he opened the door and stood there frozen with his eyes closed, expecting to feel a sharp razor's edge slitting his throat.

"Nothing happened. He opened his eyes and saw the notorious thief lying in full prostration at his feet. Perplexed, the storyteller exclaimed, 'What is this? What in the world is happening?'

The thief raised himself up and placed the bundle at the story-teller's feet. Through tears the thief said, 'I have seen the Lord, my Krishna. He gave all His ornaments to me, but I do not want any of them. They belong to you, you who inspired me to long to see my Lord. You are my Guru. Receive this and bless me.'

"Upon hearing this story which sounded utterly crazy to him, the storyteller was taken aback. He suspected that this thief, a great sinner, must have killed an innocent child and taken all his jewelry. When he exclaimed something to this effect, the thief swore that he had seen the Lord, that the Lord had placed his head on His lap and fed him with His very own hands. He further described how Krishna played such haunting melodies on His divine flute. As the storyteller listened to the thief, he noticed the ecstatic mood, the blissful tears and the excitement in his voice and thus felt something special in the man. His curiosity aroused, he opened the bundle and was absolutely amazed. Blinking several times and rubbing his eyes over and over again, he could not believe what he saw. It did not take him long to realize that these were indeed Krishna's ornaments and the thief really had had a vision of the Lord. Eyes filled with tears and a heart filled with intense longing, the storyteller called out, 'Krishna! Krishna... Am I a greater sinner than this thief?' He ran out of the house and disappeared.

"Forgoing food and sleep for several days, the storyteller reached the same spot where he had sent the thief. He fainted and regained consciousness several times over and over again. Each time he came back to normal consciousness, he ran about calling, 'Krishna, am I not worthy to behold your Divine Form? I have been singing Your glories for the last thirty years. What greater merit did the thief have to behold Your Divine Form than killing people and stealing their possessions?' Such were the prayers and supplications of the storyteller. But the Lord did not reveal

Himself to the storyteller. Immensely disappointed, the storyteller decided to commit suicide. Without having the vision of the Lord, he found no meaning in life. Now considering how fortunate the thief was to behold the Lord's enchanting form, he lost all ill feeling he had had toward the thief. But his own sincere wish to see the Lord remained unfulfilled. Greatly pained at heart, the storyteller removed his upper garment and tied one end around the branch of a tree. He climbed the tree and tied the other end around his neck. He was about to jump and hang himself when all of a sudden he heard a voice from the sky.

"It said, 'You are also very dear to Me. Console yourself. I am pleased with you, but I am not revealing My Form to you right now. Listen to Me. You wanted to know what merit the thief had to be awarded My physical presence? It was nothing but his unconditional faith that I am a reality and not just an imagination. Immediately when he heard you describe My Form, he believed that I was alive in body. He had no doubt I was a reality and was determined to see Me. His determination to see Me was so strong that it had all the qualities of real tapas. Then once he saw Me, he became mad with love. However, for you I was only a fabricated tale and not a reality. Out of fear you were even ready to deny My existence. Where there is fear, I am not. Where there is faith, there is no fear. You had no faith. But the thief had unconditional faith about My existence and about Me as a reality. It was almost mechanical for you to tell My stories and sing My glories. You never felt the longing and the desperation to see Me. At twelve o'clock sharp you wanted to eat your lunch. At eight 'on the nose' you wanted your supper and promptly at ten you went to bed—very scheduled. The thief was not like this! He forgot everything else and constantly remembered Me till he saw Me. Now be content with hearing My voice. I will bestow the blessing of appearing before you during this lifetime, but until then, go spread my message with love and devotion. It will help many other thieves, sinners and nonbelievers change their ways and become benefactors of the world.'

"Therefore, children, do not think about your dark past. Try to be determined and detached. It doesn't matter whether you were a thief or a great sinner. The Lord doesn't care about your past, provided you have determination and detachment in the present."

The wonderful healing touch of Amma

Wednesday, 15, August 1984

In the evening at about five o'clock, a family consisting of father, mother and son came to see Amma. Their son, G., a young man about eighteen years old, joyfully ran up to Br. Balu, who was standing near the backwaters. In a few moments, his father and mother came up to join them, and the family was happily talking to Balu. Seeing their pleasant and joyful mood, Balu thought, "What a tremendous transformation that's happened in their lives in the last year and a half. When they first came here, all three of them were so exhausted and drained of life. They were like corpses. Now they are cheerful with smiling faces."

This family had previously had another son besides G. The parents had been delighted in their happy family of four. The two brothers were very loving and attached to each other. G., the elder brother, always cherished and supported his younger brother, J., even though the latter was a little mischievous at times. Their love for each other was extraordinary, and they never quarreled. G. was fifteen, J. was thirteen, and they were always together. The parents were very pleased and proud of their children's concern for each other. If J. had a problem, G. sincerely tried to sort it out through his loving and affectionate ways. If J. were sick, G. would always sit by his side, tending to his needs and giving him medicine at the appropriate time. If J. did not eat, G. would refuse to eat; and vice versa. It was a strong and unusual bond which existed between the two brothers. But cruel fate did not let this last long.

One day, before the family met Amma, the younger one suddenly fell dead while playing with his brother. Later it was discovered that the cause of death was an embolism in the brain. The death occurred right in front of G.'s eyes. The boy was immediately taken to the hospital, but all was in vain. The entire family was plunged into deep sorrow. The death of his dear brother was such a shock to G. that he lapsed into unconsciousness and remained for several days in a coma. As he lay in the intensive care unit of the hospital, the parents were very worried. They were afraid that they would lose G., too. Finally, one day he opened his eyes and the parents rejoiced. But such happiness was short-lived because G. never came back to his normal self.

Although G. was alive, he was like a vegetable. He slept, but he hardly ate anything. He never talked or smiled. The boy became gaunt like a skeleton. Two years passed like this following the death of his brother. During these two years the parents tried everything—the best medical specialists were consulted; they tried various methods of therapy and different medication was administered to try to bring their boy back to normal. But all their attempts ended in failure. G. would not even blink his eyes. The despairing parents lost all hope and lived in utter hopelessness and frustration.

While the parents were leading such a life of sorrow and despair, the mother had a dream one night in which she saw a lady in white who was lovingly soothing and rubbing her son's forehead. There was a divine glow around the lady and Her compassionate smile had the power to remove all worries and wounds caused by the past. As She rubbed the boy's forehead, the lady in white called him with overflowing compassion and love, "Son... my son... Mother's darling son... my child... Look here, this is your Mother calling you." These words had a wonderful effect on the boy; he looked up at the lady's glowing face and smiled for the first time in two years. His own face was completely changed and he returned to normal. The parent's happiness knew no bounds as the mother cried and laughed out of joy. She was still in this state when her husband awoke her from her dream. Realizing that it was all a dream, the mother sobbed uncontrollably. She related the dream to her husband. Neither of them gave much thought to the dream, but the mother began to have the same dream over and over again the following nights. Since this recurring dream was happening every night, both the husband and wife began to give serious thought to it.

Because Amma was not as well known then as She became later, they were not able to find out who the lady in white was. One day as they were returning home after visiting relatives, they were waiting at a railway station to catch the next train to their town. The mother was sitting next to another woman, and after a while this woman, who was a total stranger, turned to her and spoke, "Something inside tells me that I should speak to you about Mother." The woman was Amma's devotee, and she began speaking to G.'s mother about Amma. As if she were possessed, the woman told her all about the different experiences she had had with Amma. As the woman continued speaking, the face of G.'s mother blossomed with joy. The latter realized that this woman was talking about none other than the lady in white of her dreams.

She now told the woman about what her family had been undergoing the last two years and further disclosed the recurring dream about the lady in white and that she and her husband had been trying to discover who the lady was and where they could find her, or if she even existed at all. Both the husband and wife were very happy to finally learn who Amma was and they decided to go to Mother's Ashram the very next day. As they boarded the train to their home, they began to wonder how the strange woman was inspired to talk to them about Amma for no particular reason. Had their son been with them, the woman would have seen how he looked and thus might have felt that they should take the boy to see Amma to be healed. But they did not bring the boy on this trip, having left him in the care of his aunt. Anyhow, they concluded, God's ways are incomprehensible to the human intellect.

The three of them—husband, wife and son—came to the Ashram in the morning around ten o'clock. Amma was already in the hut giving darshan. Just as they arrived and were standing in front of the temple, Br. Balu approached them and said, "Amma is calling you. Please come in." They were again surprised. Who had told Her that they were there? The family was led to Amma.

Amma smilingly said to them, "Mother was waiting for you; She knew you would come today." Amma then caught hold of the boy's hand and with a glowing smile on Her face, rubbed and soothed the boy's forehead, saying to him, "Son... my son... Look here, this is your Mother calling you..." Hearing these words, the boy slowly raised his head and gazed at the glowing, radiant face of Amma and smiled for the first time in two years. His face was completely changed; he looked as if he were coming back to normal.

The mother of the boy, who was intently watching the entire scene, cried uncontrollably and laughed out of joy. The father silently shed tears of joy. What they had just witnessed was the same scene that the boy's mother had seen in her dreams night after night. Words are inadequate to express their happiness. Later, before leaving the Ashram, the woman and her husband said, "Now we know. We have no doubts that it was all a divine drama conducted by Amma."

Day by day the boy's health and mental state improved. In a period of two months, he completely recovered from his sickness and regained his normal state of health.

While the family was still talking to Balu, Amma came down the stairs. Seeing Amma, the family rushed toward Her, calling out, "Amma, Amma!" Mother exclaimed, "Ah, children, when did you come?" She sat down on the bottom step, and after prostrating, the three gathered around Her. Amma's compassion overflowed toward them through Her loving hugs and caresses. Her soothing words of concern went directly to their hearts, and Her easy, relaxed manner made them so comfortable that they were all laughing and rejoicing together. At last G. began singing a song to Amma, and the parents joined in. Hearts filled with devotion, they all sang together

Arikil undenkilum

O Mother, even though You are near
I wander alone unable to know You,
Even though I have eyes
I still search, unable to see You.

Aren't You the beautiful moon
That blooms forth in the blue winter night?
I am like a wave that beats its head on the shore
Unable to reach the sky.

Upon understanding the Truth
That all worldly comforts are worthless,

I long to know You
As I shed tears day and night.

Oh, won't You come and comfort one
Who is so weary of the burden of sorrow?
With the desire that You will come,
I am always waiting.

At the end of the song all three burst into tears. As Mother wiped their tears with Her own hands, a loving and compassionate smile radiated from Her face. At Her feet sat the father, the mother and their son, each being caressed by the firm gentle strokes of Amma's hands. This touching scene with the family seemed to have a timeless quality about it. There sat the Eternal Mother, majestic yet welcoming all Her children. Though the day was drawing to a close, the small family was blissfully rejoicing at the dawn of Amma, the spiritual sun, in their lives.

Glossary

Certain words are the same or similar in Malayalam and Sanskrit. Thus *Abhyasa* and *Brahmachari* are Sanskrit whereas *Abhyasam* and *Brahmachari* are Malayalam

Adharma: Unrighteousness, sin, opposed to Divine Harmony.

Agamas: Scriptures.

Ammachi: Mother. Chi is a word indicating respect.

Anooraniyaan Mahatomahiyan: Sanskrit for "Subtler than the subtlest, bigger than the biggest," a description of Brahman, the Supreme Reality.

Arati: Waving the burning camphor, which leaves no residue, with ringing of bells at the end of puja (worship) indicating total annihilation of ego.

Archana: A mode of worship by repetition of one hundred, three hundred or a thousand names of the deity.

Arjuna: The third among the Pandavas and a great archer.

Ashramam: Hermitage or residence of a sage.

Atma(n): The Self

Atma bodha: Self-knowledge or Self-awareness

Avadhuta: A Realized Soul who has transcended all social conventions.

Bhagavad Gita: The teachings of Lord Krishna to Arjuna at the beginning of the Mahabharata War. It is a practical guide for common man for every day life and is the essence of Vedic wisdom. Bhagavad means 'that of the Lord' and Gita means 'Song', particularly, an advice.

Bhagavata(m): The book about the Incarnations of Lord Vishnu, especially Krishna and His childhood antics. It upholds the supremacy of devotion.

Bhagavati: The Goddess of six virtues, viz, prosperity, valor, auspiciousness, knowledge, dispassion and lordship.

Bhajan: Devotional singing

Bhakti: Devotion.

Bhava: Mood.

Bhava Darshan: The occasion when Amma receives devotees in the exalted state of the Universal Mother.

Bhrantan: Having the nature of a madman, alluding to the nature or appearance of some Realized Souls.

Brahman: The Absolute, Whole.

Brahmachari: A celibate student under training of a Guru.

Brahmacharya: Celibacy

Dakshina: Reverential offering in cash or kind.

Darshan: Audience of a Holy Person or deity.

Deva: Demi-god, celestial being

Devi: The Goddess.

Devi Bhava: Divine Mood of, or identity with, the Goddess

Devi Mahatmyam: A sacred hymn in praise of the Goddess.

Dharma: Righteousness, in accordance with Divine Harmony.

Dhritharasthra: Blind king and father of the Kauravas.

Duryodhana: Eldest son of Dhritharasthra, villain of the Mahabharata War.

Gita: Song, See Bhagavad Gita

Gopas: Cowherd boys, companions of Sri Krishna.

Gopis: Cowherd girls, known for their supreme devotion to Sri Krishna.

Guru: Spiritual Master / Guide.

Guru Paduka Stotram: Hymn of Five Verses to the Guru's Sandals.

Jagat: The ever-changing world.

Japa: Repetition of a mystical formula (mantra)

Jñana: Spiritual or divine wisdom

Kamsa: Lord Krishna's demonic uncle whom He killed.

Kanji: Rice porridge.

Kanna: Name for Krishna.

Karma: Action.

Kauravas: The hundred children of Dhritarashtra, enemies of the Pandavas, who fought in the Mahabharata War.

Kindi: Fluted metallic water pot usually used in worship.

Kirtan: Hymns

Krishna: Principle Incarnation of Lord Vishnu

Lakshmana: Brother of Lord Rama.

Lakshmi: Consort of Lord Vishnu and Goddess of wealth.

Lakshya Bodha: Constant awareness of and intent on the goal.

Lalita Sahasranama: Thousand names of the Universal Mother in the form of Lalitambika

Leela: Divine play.

Mahabharata: Great epic written by Vyasa.

Mahatma: Great Soul

Mantra: Sacred formula, the repetition of which can awaken one's spiritual energies and bring the desired results.

Maya: Illusion.

Mol: Daughter. Mole is the vocative form.

Mon: Son. Mone is the vocative form

Mudra: A sign by hand indicating mystic spiritual truths.

Mukta: The Liberated One

Mukti: Liberation.

Namah Shivaya: The Panchakshara Mantra (mantra consisting of five letters) meaning "Salutations to the Auspicious One (Shiva)."

Om: Mystical syllable representing the Supreme Reality.

Pandavas: The five children of King Pandu and heroes of the epic Mahabharata

Prarabdha: Responsibilities or burdens. Also, the fruits of past actions manifesting as the present life.

Prasad: Consecrated offerings distributed after puja.

Prema: Deep Love.

Puja: Worship.

Rama: Hero of the epic Ramayana. An incarnation of Vishnu and the ideal of Righteousness.

Ravana: The villain of the Ramayana

Rishi: A great sage or seer.

Sad-asad-rupa dharini: One who dons the form of existence and non-existence, a name of the Divine Mother.

Sadhak: One dedicated to attaining the spiritual goal, one who practices sadhana (spiritual discipline).

Sadhana: Spiritual practices.

Sahasranama: Hymns consisting of the Thousand Names of God.

Samadhi: State of absorption in the Self.

Samsara: The world of plurality, the cycle of birth and death.

Samskaras: Mental tendencies accumulated from past actions.

Sankalpa: Creative, integral resolve manifesting as thought, feeling and action. The sankalpa of an ordinary person does not always bear corresponding fruit. The sankalpa of a sage, however, always bears the intended result.

Sannyasi(n): Ascetic who has renounced all worldly bondages.

Satguru: Realized Spiritual Master.

Satsang: Company of the wise and virtuous. Also, a spiritual discourse by a sage or scholar.

Shakti: The dynamic aspect of Brahman as the Universal Mother.

Shiva: The static aspect of Brahman as the male principle.

Sishya: Disciple.

Sita: Wife of Rama.

Sloka: Sanskrit verse.

Sraddha: Faith. Amma uses it with a special emphasis on alertness coupled with loving care of the work in hand.

Sri Rama: See Rama. Sree, or Sri, is a mark of respect

Srimad Bhagavatam: See Bhagavatam. Srimad means 'auspicious'

Stenah: Thief.

Sutra: Aphorism.

Tapas: Literally "heat." The practice of spiritual austerities.

Tapasvi: One engaged in penance or spiritual austerities.

Tapovan(am): Hermitage, a place conducive to meditation and tapas.

Tattva: Principle.

Upanishads: The concluding portion of the Vedas dealing with the philosophy of Non-dualism.

Vasana: Latent tendency.

Veda: Lit. 'Knowledge', the authoritative Scriptures of the Hindus.

Veda Vyasa: See Vyasa. As he divided the one Veda into four, he is also known by the name of Veda Vyasa

Vedanta(m): The philosophy of the Upanishads which declare the Ultimate Truth as 'One without a Second.'

Vedantin: A follower of the Vedanta philosophy.

Vedic Dharma: Injunctions on the righteous way of living as prescribed by the Vedas.

Vidyavidya svarupini: Whose nature is knowledge andignorance, a name of the Divine Mother.

Vishnu: All-pervading. The Lord of sustenance.

Vyasa: A sage who divided the one Veda into four and composed 18 Puranas and also the Mahabharata and Bhagavatam.

Index

A

adharma 88
animals
    feeding with love 13
apathy 116
atma bodha 38
attachment 163
    attachment to the Guru 49, 129
attitude
    Guru-sishya relationship 177
    right attitude for devotees 48, 215

B

bhakti 50
Bhima 62

C

compassion 55, 88
concentration 20, 35
crying to God 34, 84

D

Dakshinamurti 17
desires
    desires and peace 68
    desires of a Mahatma 13
    desire and prayer 36
    intense desire and love 20
    renunciation of desires 201
destiny 79, 138
detachment 102, 163, 191, 202
devotees

right attitude for devotees 48
doubts 43, 147
Duryodhana 145, 164

E

ego 31, 34, 145, 153, 161, 163, 175, 176, 190
    as seen by saints 93
    discipline with and without ego 176
empathy 13
experience 16, 21, 23, 40, 71, 105, 165, 201

F

faith 42, 69, 89, 147, 148, 217
    nonbelievers and faith 86
fear 142, 217
    Mahatmas and fear 138
forgetting
    attachment to the Guru and forgetting 49
    concentration and forgetting 52
    crying and forgetting 35
    forgetting the past 216
forgiveness 143, 152, 176, 177
    Mother's forgiveness 216

G

Ganges 31, 64, 133
Gayatri 33, 48, 55, 88, 124
God 119, 202
    attitude that Mother is God 54
    God's grace 28, 79, 81, 216
    knowing God 34
    remembering God 27, 65, 216
    serving God 193, 194, 195
Gopis 34, 50, 53, 103
grace 35, 79
gratitude
    expecting gratitude for service 194

Guru 46, 212
    attachment to the Guru 49, 129
    Guru-sishya relationship 176
    Guru's grace 79, 206
    Guru's guidance 206
    imitation of the Guru 132
    obedience to the Guru 83, 121, 132
Gurudakshina 180
Guru Paduka Stotram 78

H

Harshan 130
heart 16, 27, 44, 69, 117
helplessness 35, 190
humility 35, 194

I

ignorance 94
intellect 16, 41, 69, 146
    beyond the intellect 84, 105, 134, 137

J

Jarasandha 62
Jesus 62, 150, 213
Judas 213

K

Kaikeyi 151
Kamsa 145
karma 79
Krishna 50, 62, 152, 164, 217

L

lakshya bodha 215
Lalita Sahasranama 132
logic 41, 69, 73

love 13, 27, 34, 42, 44, 45, 49, 57, 60, 69, 154, 158, 174
    work with love 109, 191

M

Maanikkavaachakar 210
Mahatmas 86, 118, 119, 137, 153, 179
    desires 13
    following society's rules and regulations 132
    Mahatma's body 61, 62
    their compassion 57, 134
meditation 17, 27, 100, 101, 109, 162
    crying to God 27, 32, 34
    remembrance of God 49
mind 43, 91, 134
    mind and desires 68
    no-mind 58
    one-pointed mind 15, 35
    purifying the mind 31
    stillness of mind 16, 20, 23, 201
Mirabai 34
Mother
    healing 60, 189
    Her desires 203, 205
    Her samadhi states 23, 88, 110, 111, 185
    Mother's ashram 116
    Mother's concern for the welfare of her neighbors 74, 173
    Mother's life 156
    Mother's sankalpa 77, 133
    Mother's work 133, 156
    Mother and the owl 55
    Mother answers seekers' call 115
    Mother as Brahman 54
Mother - in Her own words
    Her desires 197
    Her ego 215
    Mother's body 115
    Mother's compassion 134

Mother's role in Her children's spiritual growth 215
Mother's sankalpa 133
Mother as Brahman 54
Mother and Her children
    feeding Her children 123
    in previous births 81
    playing with Her children 127
    work 109, 191, 199

N

Narada 50, 85
Naranattu Bhrantan 135
Narasimha 28
nonbelievers 86, 145

O

obedience 121
offerings 35, 64, 195

P

Parvati 17
past
    effects of past actions on a seeker 152, 216
    healing the past 225, 226
    learning from the past 167
    thinking about the past 68, 92
peace 68, 104
penetration 83
prarabdha 138
prayer 27, 35, 189, 190
prema 32

R

Rama 62, 145, 151, 164
Ravana 145, 151, 164
reaction 146, 176

remembering 65
    remembering God 27, 34, 216
    with discrimination 167, 168
renunciation 40
    of desires 201
    of Mahatmas 86, 180
rishis 22, 24, 105

S

sad-asad-rupa dharini 132
sadhana 14, 27, 32, 194
    Gayatri's sadhana 49
    Mirabai's and the Gopis' sadhana 34
saints 44, 85, 93, 122, 180
samskara 87
sankalpa 58, 60
    Mother's sankalpa 77, 133
Satguru
    Satguru's grace 206
    Satguru's will 38
science 20, 41, 70, 71, 147
seeker 13, 14, 131, 170, 194
    Mother answers seekers' call 115
service 109, 194
    selfless service 60
Shiva 17, 201, 202
silence 16, 100, 104, 201
sishya 176
slokas
    Bhagavad Gita 102
    Shankaracharya 187
speech 16
spirituality 26, 86, 192, 201, 215
    writing about spirituality 105
sraddha 89
stillness 16, 40, 58, 91, 201
stories

Baby Krishna, the storyteller, and the thief 217
Buddha's compassion 58
Krishna's headache 50
Narada, Vishnu, and the childless couple 85
Naranattu Bhrantan and his disciple 135
Naranattu Bhrantan and the demigoddess 136
the Gopi who burned her fingers 53
the healthy beggar 118
the Mahatma and the hooligan 152
the Mahatma and the millionaire 195
the Mahatma who gave away toys and sweets 40
the painters' competition to paint peace 104
the sadhak and the forest dweller 28
the thief and the rich man 90
the vengeful king and the compassionate guru 180
the villager, the sannyasin, and the diamond 202
Veda Vyasa and the Gopis 103
surrender 35, 69, 142, 190

T

tears 27, 31, 34, 57
thoughts 16, 20, 58, 65, 92, 133, 162, 192, 197, 209

U

urgency 46, 60, 147

V

vasanas 35, 38, 87, 132, 146, 206
Vedanta 32
Veda Vyasa 103
vidyavidya svarupini 132
Vishnu 28, 85

W

wealth 90, 196
witness consciousness 99

work 19, 65, 109, 164, 191, 199
    Mother's work 133, 156
    work of a saint 60, 100, 122, 134, 138